The author, Abdullahi Osman Mohamed, was born, studied and worked in Somalia. He had also worked in the Arabian Gulf. Later, he studied in London and finally he settled and started working in Bolton, North West England, where he is currently living with his family.

The author had worked with children in a school in Bolton for a long time. He has recently retired from work. Having an abundant culture and life experience, he loves writing fiction and non-fiction stories. Since he speaks few foreign languages, he likes reading memoirs in different languages and true stories that are inspirational to others.

I dedicate this book to my father, Osman Mohamed, who intiated my education when he took me to a quran school in a village. In addition, he did anything that he could to help me to be successful in this life and the hereafter. May Allah forgive all of his sins.

Abdullahi Osman Mohamed

An Adventurous Life

Austin Macauley Publishers
LONDON · CAMBRIDGE · NEW YORK · SHARJAH

Copyright © Abdullahi Osman Mohamed 2024

The right of Abdullahi Osman Mohamed to be identified as author of this work has been asserted by the author in accordance with sections 77 and 78 of the Copyright, Designs and Patents Act 1988.

All rights reserved. No part of this publication may be reproduced, stored in a retrieval system, or transmitted in any form or by any means, electronic, mechanical, photocopying, recording, or otherwise, without the prior permission of the publishers.

Any person who commits any unauthorised act in relation to this publication may be liable to criminal prosecution and civil claims for damages.

All of the events in this memoir are true to the best of the author's memory. The views expressed in this memoir are solely those of the author.

A CIP catalogue record for this title is available from the British Library.

ISBN 9781035816866 (Paperback)
ISBN 9781035816873 (ePube-book)

www.austinmacauley.com

First Published 2024
Austin Macauley Publishers Ltd®
1 Canada Square
Canary Wharf
London
E14 5AA

I would like to thank all my friends and family members who encouraged me to write the stories in this book. Also, your help was invaluable and without it this amazing work wouldn't have been published successfully.

Table of Contents

Chapter One: Childhood Adventure	11
Chapter Two: Rural Development Adventure	34
Chapter Three: A Teacher's Adventure	47
Chapter Four: Risk-Taking Adventure	76
Chapter Five: Arabian Desert Adventure	81
Chapter Six: The Brutal Somali Civil War (Black Hawk Down)	106
Chapter Seven: Scramble to Djibouti Adventure	122
Chapter Eight: Travel Abroad Adventure	136
Chapter Nine: UK Life Adventure	148

Chapter One
Childhood Adventure

Humans are created individually and everyone is unique, just like their fingerprints. Every human being has their character and personality. Likewise, they take their own path in life that is different from anyone else. Even identical twins, who share the same womb and birthdate, are unique individuals. They might look alike but they are uniquely created and are different from each other. Just like any other human being, they take their own path in life and try to make their own decisions and act upon them. Some of the human life stories are interesting and outstanding.

The adventurous life stories you are about to read are about an individual who is kindly willing to disclose most of his interesting experiences in his life. He is quite sure that the stories will benefit the readers in many different ways.

In this world, there are countless, amazing life stories that are similar to this, but unfortunately, a very small number of people are able to write their stories and share them with the world. The writer believes he is privileged to be one of those who can do so.

My name is Abdullah Osman Mohamed. I was born in Somalia, in the wilderness of the countryside in a district called El-Bur. Due to a lack of records in the countryside my date of birth has never been known. I was told that I was born around the years 1954 or 1955. My date of birth was not a concern to me until it was a requirement for me to have one. When I was asked about my date of birth, the only solution was to make one up. Since I had the choice, I chose the latter year, to keep myself one year younger. My family used to have some camels and goats. I remember we used to move from one area of the countryside to another, looking for water and grazing for our animals.

To view how the Somali nomadic life is, see this video. **Nomad boy (1960) a great Somali documentary. YouTube.**

When I was around seven years old, my father Osman Mohamed wanted me to learn the Quran which was the only and the most popular education programme that was available in that area. He took me to a village where there was a Quran teacher, who taught some children from the village. Since we were nomads, who moved from one area to another, my family couldn't live in the village. So, my father asked the teacher to let me stay in the village with him. I remember my father gave me some beans in a small cloth bag and a small cooking pot. I stayed in the hut where the children and I were taught how to read and write the Arabic writing and then the Quran.

I started learning how to read and write the Quran. My father used to come to see me regularly and brought some more beans for me to eat.

It wasn't very long when droughts started to hit in the area where my family lived. The drought became extremely harsh and negatively impacted on the level of rainfall. Then our family and their livestock couldn't find anything to eat. As a result, we had to move far away from there.

Unfortunately, it was time for me to leave the hut where I took my Quran lessons. The reason was, my father would not be able to visit me due to the migration my family had to make. The short time I spent learning the Quran was beneficial. I felt lucky and grateful to my father, as this was the beginning of my learning journey.

I was around seven and a half years old when my father decided to take me to a district that was very far from home, where my paternal aunt and her family lived. We travelled by night in a big lorry full of people and their belongings. It was very dark in the countryside. The road was incredibly rough. It was so bumpy, that made people in the lorry scared due to the danger we faced. We nearly had an accident. Luckily, we arrived at a district called Beledwyne safely, where my paternal aunt lived. The family welcomed us. My aunt had many grown-up children who lived and worked in that town and Mogadishu, the capital city of Somalia.

After having a conversation with my father, my aunt decided to take me to Mogadishu, where many of her grown-up children, who had their own families lived. My aunt, my father, and I took a coach from Beledwyne to Mogadishu. It took a whole day for us to reach Mogadishu. It was sunset when we arrived in the city. To me, it was amazing, for I had never been to a city before. As a little nomadic boy, I was extremely surprised by the number of people I saw in the crowded marketplace in the city with so many vehicles in the streets. I vividly remember taking a red and yellow-coloured taxi to my aunt's children's house. It was a joyous meeting and a warm welcome.

After two weeks or so, my father had to go back to our family in the countryside. That journey back must have been very long and difficult for my father alone. I am sure that he felt he had accomplished a mission of saving one of his sons from the perilous life of the drought-ridden countryside. I am also certain that he had the ambition for me to strive for education when I started to uncover the difference between the city's life and the countryside.

One day, I went to a market with a young lady working as a domestic work assistant with my aunt's family. We were walking on a hill overlooking the Indian Ocean in the distance. Since I had never seen the sea, I thought it was a desert, in which some white goats were trying to graze. When I asked her about it, she laughed constantly and told me it was the Indian Ocean and the white goats were the sea waves.

After a few months, my aunt and I moved to another house, joining two unmarried children of hers. They were studying at high school. To them, I was a nomad boy who was brought to be looked after and be saved from the unbearable life of the countryside. I was glad and very lucky as I felt life was much easier in the city than it was in the countryside.

At least a year or so had passed. I got to know the children from the neighbourhood. At first, it wasn't easy speaking to them, but later I found it fun to have some conversations with children of my age. After a while, I realised that they were not around in the morning and I only saw them in the afternoon. "Where do they go in the morning?" I wondered. When I asked them this question, they told me they went to school in the mornings.

That reminded me of the time when I was learning the Quran and memorising it. I decided to ask them if I could attend school with them. They told me that it was possible and that the school took some new children at the beginning of each year. They also explained that the new children should know how to read the Quran and at least memorised the 30th chapter. I was delighted to hear that as I had memorised the 29th and 30th chapters when I was learning the Quran two years ago. This made me feel that there was a chance for me to attend the school they go to. After hearing this exciting information, I hurried to my aunt to share the good news with her. Unfortunately, when she heard what I had to say, she was not impressed.

I am not quite sure about what she was thinking of at that time. However, there is one thing I can imagine she thought of. There was some sort of cost in taking a child to school. My aunt and her two unmarried children were relying financially on her other working, married children.

Since I wasn't encouraged by my aunt, it wasn't easy to carry on having thoughts of going to school next year.

Imagine, a boy of that age wandering around in his area on his own, when all the other children had gone to school. I felt helpless and miserable at those times. I decided to walk around the area. Sometimes I went a bit far from the area where our house was, to discover the parts of the city. I was also mindful of being lost.

When I went far from the area I knew well, it reminded me of a day when I got lost in the countryside years ago. After realising I was missing, my parents started to look for me and found me hours later. It was a terrifying time in my life as a wild animal could have found me and ate me. Being reminded of that horrifying experience many years ago, I said to myself, "I shouldn't go any further," and returned to the area I knew well.

After being alone all morning, I used to see the children return from school in the afternoon which instantly changed my mood as we all played together. We played football and other games that kept us busy until the evening, when we had to go home, eat and go to sleep. Sometimes whilst playing, my feet would hurt and bled as I didn't have shoes. The marks are on my feet to this day, but it didn't matter to me at the time due to the amount of fun and excitement I felt whilst playing football with the children from the neighbourhood.

Even though I wasn't given any encouragement to find a school, I did not forget the idea of finding it myself. I kept asking the children when the beginning of the school year was. Finally, they told me that it wasn't long. I began to ponder about it and came up with some ideas of how I could attend school myself. I asked myself about the Quran I had to know by heart and if they would ask me to recite it by heart. It was around two years ago since I had memorised it and I had not practised since then, which was a problem. So I decided to find the holy Quran and start reading it again. At first, I couldn't find it in the house I lived in, but then, I went to my cousin's house, and there I found the holy Quran, then I began revising what I once memorised a few years ago.

Imagine a boy of fewer than ten years of age working hard to find an education by himself with no one giving a hand or any mental encouragement, trying to fulfil the requirements to attend school on his own.

After a long wait that felt ages, it was finally the day when the school was taking in the new children. Being alone, I made my way to the school that was not far from where I lived. Many children with their parents filled the front area of the school.

After a while, the children including me were asked to come into the school and entered the classes. Then, a teacher started to ask each child to recite the Quran by heart. It was then my turn and I was told to recite the 30th chapter. After a few minutes of reciting, the teacher stopped me and wrote my name in a book. Knowing I made no mistakes, that could only have meant that he was satisfied with the quality of my recitation. That filled me with excitement, as I was convinced that I had passed the test to enrol in the school.

After many days of waiting, we finally returned to the school to find out the results of the test and who could enrol in the school. A teacher stood at the gate of the school and started calling out the names of the children who passed the test. To my extreme delight, my name was called and I rushed into the school. A teacher inside the school greeted us and helped us line up before taking some of us into the classes. Some parents stood beside our lines and they were speaking to the teachers. Many children were then taken out of the lines, they put them into the classrooms and a few children were left out including me. Sadly, we were told that there were no places for us somehow. My hope and dreams were ripped away. I felt cheated and unfairly treated.

I ran to my aunt and told her the horrible news and she also felt unhappy about it. After a few days, there came into the house one of my aunt's sons who worked as a teacher for the department of education, in a very far district from

Mogadishu. My aunt asked him to help me attend that school. It was a school day, my cousin and I immediately made our way to the school while it was open. We entered the school and headed to the head teacher's office. I was told to wait outside the office while my cousin went in and spoke to the head teacher. After a while, my cousin exited the office and told me that I couldn't attend the school as it was full and there were no places left. That made me sad. Despite being disappointed about the result of my endeavour, I had not given up on my dream of attending a school, so I kept thinking about what I could do next.

In the days after being rejected by the school, there were some English tuition lessons taking place in our house. A young lady, who was my aunt's daughter, started to help her nephews to do their English homework. They were more or less of my age. This was an opportunity for me to see what the children were learning at school. Soon, I realised that what they were learning was a foreign language. I kept watching and listening as it was interesting to me.

I asked some of the children in my neighbourhood if they knew any other school in the area. One of them told me that there was a new school in an area that was quite far from the area where we lived. However, after asking some more questions on how to get there and the name of the school, I was confident that I could go there safely and see what I could do.

I remember it was in the morning, around 10AM when I started my unpredictable walking endeavour to find the new school. On my way I was asking people on the road where the new school was. A few people knew where it was and gave me some directions to find it. I kept walking towards it.

After walking a few miles, I met some children who were playing football. I asked them if they knew about the school I was looking for. They pointed to a building that looked like it had just been built. They told me it was the school. I asked them if this school was taking any new children. They said that there was a day set for new pupils to be tested and they would start that school year.

Finding a school was good news that had restored my hope. However, a few moments later, I realised how far I had walked away from the area I lived. As a nomad boy, I knew there was going to be some difficulty in finding my way back.

As I made my way back, I tried to recognise things and places I saw on my way here to figure out the direction I came from. It wasn't easy at all. I felt panic and fear at times I felt lost. After a long walk that felt like decades, I somehow managed to return home. I saw my aunt in the house and told her the great news. She smiled and asked me how I found it. I told her my adventurous story which made her appreciate what kind of a boy I was.

The day I had to attend school had come around. It was in the afternoon. After I had my lunch, I left the house and made my way to the school. Many children came with their parents but of course, I was alone as usual. All the children were then told to go into the classrooms. A teacher came into the class I was in, and started to test us. This time round there was no Quran recitation, but instead the teacher wrote some Arabic words on the blackboard and asked each child to read them. For me, it was very easy as I knew how to read the Quran which is written in Arabic. However, there were a few kids who struggled to read.

In the end, we were all allowed to be enrolled in year one of primary school. We were told that we needed to bring our writing books and pencils the next day. We were told that the school uniform was also necessary for everyone as soon as possible. I hurried and ran as fast as I could, to break the joyous news to my aunt. My aunt smiled and her face was lit up, and felt extremely proud of me, and she appreciated how I did it all alone.

Imagine the happiness I felt that day. For me, it was a great breakthrough after all the hard work I put in to find a school I could attend to pursue my dream in education.

The next morning, my aunt went to a shop and bought a book and a pencil for me. At last, there I was, holding a book and a pencil, going to school that afternoon. "What a success," I thought as I rushed to school. The class had started and the teacher was teaching Arabic in the first lesson. I found the lesson very easy. It was interesting due to the learning environment I was in. After that, we had maths, which was quite new to me but I didn't struggle with it. I put all my effort and attention to understand everything the teacher was explaining. From that day on, things went very well.

One day, I was in my class when the teacher called me to his desk and asked me for my birth certificate and other papers. I told him that I didn't know what they were and I didn't know where to find them. He continued and told me to tell my parents to find those papers for me.

When I came home that evening, I asked my aunt what the teacher asked me to bring. My aunt didn't know how to find those papers. So, she had to ask her children. They told us that a birth certificate was very hard for me to have as I wasn't born in a hospital.

Few weeks passed, when one of my aunt's older children came. She asked him if he could find those papers for me. He knew about those papers as he had some children who were around my age. However, he was unsure about how he could find those papers for me.

A few more weeks passed when one day a teacher called me to her desk. "Where is your uniform?" She asked.

I didn't know what to say to her but I promised that I would try to attend school wearing it. By the way, I was the only pupil in the class who was without a uniform.

Despite the excellent luck that I was blessed with, there I was facing some more challenges. Thinking about the uniform, I knew it would be hard to find the money to buy a pair of blue shorts and a white shirt, accompanied by a pair of school shoes.

My aunt was already struggling to find some money for our living. She had already bought me a pencil and a few books and she told me the other day that she owed the shopkeeper the money for the pencil and the books. Therefore I knew I couldn't ask her for the uniform.

One month or so passed, when the teacher asked me again about the uniform. I made some excuses and he let me sit down. In my class, I was one of those whom the teachers praised when it came to learning, so the uniform was not a big issue to them as they were happy about my attitude towards learning.

Weeks and months passed and finally, it was the end of year one in my primary school. At home, my cousin's children were having English language tuition by my aunt's daughter. This was a good chance for me, as I would pay attention to those English tuition lessons. I was able to write and read some basic English language, which was not taught in year one of primary school. Those children continued to attend the tuition lessons over the school holiday. Unlike the other children, who enjoyed being away from school, I found the school holidays very long and boring. For me, attending the school was interesting and couldn't wait for the new school year to begin.

Finally, the school year started but I was a little nervous on the first day. I did not have the school uniform due to the financial constraints we were still facing as a family and the birth certificate document that I didn't have. All of the children at school were filled with excitement for the new school year to begin. In the first year, we were taught how to read and write Arabic language and math in Arabic. In year two, we began learning how to read and write English. I found the lessons very easy thanks to my cousin's English tuition lessons at home.

I remember our female English teacher, whose nephew was also in our class quickly realised how good I was in the English language she was teaching. Then she decided to place her nephew next to me, and asked me to help him when he needed me.

A few weeks went by when one morning our teacher called me to his desk and asked me about the uniform and the papers. Knowing that I was at his desk and far from the other kids, I decided to uncover the truth as to why I couldn't have the papers and the uniform.

I said, "My parents are not in the city and I love learning."

He knew how good of a learner I was, so he let me stay in the class.

A few months passed and everything was going smoothly when one morning our English teacher called me to come to her. To me, it was not surprising because I always feared the question of my uniform and papers that kept coming.

This time I was only asked about the papers. Then I told her that my parents were nomad people so it would be pretty much impossible for me to get hold of a birth certificate. After that, she let me sit down. I thought she had felt some sympathy for me and turned a blind eye to my situation.

I remember one day in year two, it was a maths test day. When we were ready to receive our test papers, our maths teacher called me and told me to sit down on an edge of the wooden platform under the blackboard. She told me to do my maths test there, using my lap as a desk. It was obvious that she was trying to avoid other children to copy my work.

In year two, I had no more problems and it ended with success. Also my results were very good. At the end of that school year, my cousin who used to do tuition for me and her nephews at home had finished high school and got a job in the city centre. She started working for Somali Airlines. The family decided to move to a house somewhere near the city centre where she was working.

For me, the move was not good at all, because to go to my school, I had to walk three times the distance I used to walk and come back early in the afternoon when it was hot which I found extremely difficult. When my third school year started, my aunt was able to buy me a school uniform as her daughter started working which made our financial situation better.

Even though I lived very far from my school, I wasn't discouraged from my learning which I thought was the only way to better my life and my family in the countryside. I used to wake up early in the morning and get ready due to the long distance I had to walk. This time my aunt was well aware of the distance from home to school, so she used to make me breakfast very early in the morning. May Allah grant her his paradise and forgive all of her sins. Ameen.

I remember I used to run as fast as I could to get to school in time. When my Arabic teacher found out that I was coming from the city centre, he asked me where my area was. I told him El-Gab, an area that is very well known in Mogadishu, the capital of Somalia and my school was Casa-Popolare school which was at that time in the outskirts of Mogadishu very far from where I lived. It was hard to believe for him.

Then he said to the class, "Anyone who comes after the El-Gab boy will not enter the class."

He said so because our first lesson in the morning was the Arabic language. For me, the comment from my Arabic teacher was recognition of the hardship; I was willing to go through for my education. The recognition made me work harder and more committed.

In year three, I had my school uniform on, so I didn't stand out like before which made me feel relieved and a bit prouder of myself. Many thanks, to my aunt and her daughter.

Months went by and I worked harder and harder until one early morning, I got ready, grabbed my books, and hurried to go to school as usual. I suddenly stopped as I saw a big military tank parked across the street. Armed soldiers were stopping the traffic. I was frightened and wondered "What is happening?" One of the soldiers saw me passing by and noticed my school uniform then he said loudly, "Stop, are you going to school?"

"Yes," I responded to him.

"There is no school today," he said.

I looked at him with disbelief without saying a word because I had never seen a soldier stopping pupils from going to school and I asked myself, "What do they have to do with my school?"

He was armed with an AK47 machine gun strapped around his shoulder and was looking at me very attentively with his eyes wide open. He realised that I was not going back quickly so he shouted again, "There is no school today, understood?"

I had no choice but to nod and go back home and break the news to my aunt.

Two hours later, we found out that it was a day that there was a massive change to the Somali government. There had been a military coup that took over the Somali government. It was on 21 October 1969. I remember that day, in the afternoon, the streets were filled with people marching and chanting joyous slogans, which I couldn't understand because of my age at that time. I could only understand that people were very happy with what happened. Since there was no fight or any altercations, everything went back to normal very soon.

Back to my school's story, my routine was back to normal. Wake up very early in the morning, run as fast as I could to school, come home sweating from the extreme heat in the early afternoon. With all these difficulties, I never gave up. Enthusiastic as I was, to me it was only a good experience.

My English teacher in year two was teaching my class in year three too. She found out that this year I was coming to school from the city centre. She told me that some children of hers were going to a high school in the city centre in the afternoon and their house was near our school. She kindly offered me to go in their car with them. I couldn't thank her enough and I was so grateful.

From that day on to the end of year three, I had that ride in the afternoon. So, there I was in the car, opening the car windows enjoying the glorious Indian Ocean's breeze. This was a direct contrast to what I used to feel from walking to school in the morning then going back in the afternoon, sweating, thirsty and tired. For me, it was something I could never dream of.

After I had finished year three, in the school holidays, I started to get to know some of the children in my new area. I asked them if they knew a primary school around the area. They told me there was one. I was thinking of getting transferred to the nearby school but I couldn't figure out how to. I could have asked my aunt but I knew she would have had to ask others for help, so I decided to try my hardest before telling anyone. After having many thoughts, I had concluded to go to the school on my own and ask the head teacher if they had a place for me in the school.

After the school holidays, the schools were opened, I went to the school in my area, and I asked the head teacher.

To my delight, he told me they had a place for me. I was overwhelmed with joy and excitement.

The next day, when I went to my school, I told my teacher that I found a place in a school in my area, so I wanted my results of the past years to attend that school. After having a word with my head teacher, they decided to give me my results. When the head teacher got my results from the files, he had a look at my marks from the results of the past three years. He looked at me and said, "What a good boy!" My marks were all 8 out of 10, 9 out of 10, or 10 out of 10. They were never lower than those. The head teacher handed me the certificate and said, "If they don't give you a place, you can come back here."

I thanked him and went home.

I informed my aunt about what I did, she was proud of me. In the next morning, I was at the head teacher's office of the new school. The school was called Moalim Jama Primary and Middle school. I handed in my certificate from my previous school. Then I was enrolled in year four, the final year of primary school.

Luckily, I didn't have to buy a new school uniform, because all the primary schools had the same uniforms: A white shirt and a pair of blue shorts.

"A fresh new start in a school so close to my house," I happily thought. At first, it was a very good start with no problems, but after a few months, I was asked about my birth certificate and one more document. I told them that I didn't know how to find them.

A few more months passed. I was doing well in my studies until one day; I was called to the office. They told me that the school had to prepare the papers of the year four pupils and send them to the Ministry of Education well before the final examination. They added that, if I didn't get those papers I would not be included in the pupils who were taking part in the exam.

"What a dreadful news that is!" I thought.

Think of how it all started. The ups and downs I had, when I had to find a school all on my own, and no one to help me. I was the odd one out as I was lacking uniform whilst all the other students were very well dressed in their uniforms. I was running for miles, and miles every morning and afternoon. It was depressing to find myself in that situation.

I went home with very little hope. I told my aunt about what the teacher had told me. I sat down next to her on a mat and I looked down with sorrow and despair. She would normally see me busy with my studies and being very happy reading my books and not playing outside. She knew that education and learning were the keys for a good life and a good future for children like me. Her children were all literate and worked hard learning and earning some money for their families.

My aunt's husband died a long time ago, so she brought up her children on her own. I was told that her children were all born in the countryside where my family lived before my father got married. Even though my aunt was married with children and husband, they didn't have their own animals or farm. So, they were part of her father's family. My father was much younger than her and used to help my aunt bring her babies up because her husband used to go away for a long time and come back and go again, then he never stayed permanently. Then he died very far away from home.

When some of her children were in their teens, my grandfather died in a tribal war in the countryside and all the family's camels were robbed in that war. I was told that my grandfather used to own over a hundred camels and my father (a young single man then) used to look after the camels. I can imagine when my aunt was having her children; she didn't have to worry about feeding them when her husband was away because a family with a hundred camels was really rich.

After that terrible tribal war happened, the family became poor. Then my aunt decided to move to Hiiraan's capital city Beledweyne with her children, and then they started a new life there. I can imagine how hard it was for my aunt and her children to start a new life in a city whilst being from the countryside. I can also imagine what they went through. To me, it was an amazing achievement that a nomadic family who moved to the city managed to earn living and educate themselves then started working for the government.

In Mogadishu, I remember when my father visited us, my aunt used to show great respect and appreciation for my father. She always mentioned the great help he used to give her children, whilst looking after the hundred camels that the whole family was relying on. First and foremost were my aunt and her ten children, while her husband used to come and go away.

That time, it was my family who needed help, and that was why my aunt was mentioning how helpful my father used to be when her children were growing up.

For me, it was really helpful to have some relatives in the city, because even though the attention they paid to my education was minimal, my journey to education and even living in the city would have been impossible without them. I say minimal attention was paid to my education because no one had even been to the schools I attended to see the progress I was making or any problems I had.

Back to my school story, there we were my aunt and I sat side by side not knowing what to do next. Both my aunt and I were speechless thinking of the documents the teachers asked for. After minutes of silence, my aunt patted on my shoulder and said to me, "Let us rely on Allah and do what we can."

We Muslims believe that Allah had already planned everything for us, and they will happen as planned, but we don't know when and how they will happen. We also believe that Allah knows what's best for us. So, when things like that happen we calm ourselves down and remember that no matter how hard things get to deal with, we have to have faith in Allah and believe that we will only get what Allah had planned for us. That doesn't mean sit down and wait; but it means, do what you can and wait relying on Allah's final decision.

Later that day in the evening, one of my aunt's two daughters came to us. My aunt told her about my hard work in the school for the past four years, and the books and pens and the uniform all were going to go wasted. While they were talking, I was listening to them. My aunt was explaining the serious situation that we were in. Her daughter showed full understanding of the situation and she stayed for a while, then she went back to her house.

My aunt's daughter came back to us the next morning and told me to come with her. I got ready and looked at her. She said to me, "We will try something."

At the time, she was working for the Ministry of Justice as a secretary. She took me to a court. The people who were working there knew her well because she was the secretary of the Minister of Justice. They greeted and welcomed her. I remember the nice words they said to her, "It's very nice to see you. How can we help you today?"

I was sure that she was glad to hear that, as she had a problem to solve. She spoke to the judge of the court and explained the problem to him. She told him that I was her cousin and my parents were not living in the city. She added that she took care of me but because of my school, I needed some documents like a birth certificate. She also clarified further that I wasn't born in the city. In the end, they decided that she had to write a statement, stating that she was my relative carer. My name and a made-up date of birth were written on the statement. The judge told her that she needed two witnesses to sign her statement. There were some people at the court, so she asked two men to witness and sign the statement for her, which they did. After that, the judge signed and approved it. From there on, I didn't know how much more work was remaining but I could see the relief on my cousin's face.

At that moment, I felt like I was being rescued from the deep waters of a sea to safety on the land. My cousin looked at me and said, "Let's go."

We walked and walked to the Municipal Office. In the Municipal Office, she explained what she wanted, and handed the statement to them. They found her family's file, and then they wrote my name under the list of her children. They also put the statement in her file. They gave me the number of her family file and told me to bring a photo of myself the next day. They told me that they would give me an ID. Subsequently, I could have any documents I needed. AMAZING! I couldn't believe what I was hearing.

I asked myself quietly, "How many years have I been waiting for this." I hugged her and there were tears of joy in my eyes. That was an unforgettable day in my life. I found hope once again. I was determined to work harder in my studies. While we were walking back home, I held my head high proudly.

When we reached home, my aunt heard the news and was extremely relieved. She made the most sincere (Duas), asking Allah to give her daughter the best reward.

From that day on, I got on with my learning. The next day, I went to school being proud of myself and having high hopes.

When I was in year five, I had a little fight with a boy in my class and our teacher saw us fighting then he shouted at us and told us to bring our parents otherwise we were not allowed to come to the school.

As my parents were not in the city and I couldn't tell my aunt being ashamed of myself, I thought of an idea. I told one of my older friends to come with me to the school, pretending to be my older brother. I told him to slap me in front of the teacher after he had listened to what the teacher had to say about me. The next day, I brought my friend with me, he listened to what the teacher had to say and he slapped me in the face. The teacher was convinced that I would not do it again, and then he let me go into my class. Despite the pain on my face, I was glad that my plan had worked.

Everything was normal until the beginning of year seven. I had heard that my family in the countryside was moving to Beledweyne. Beledweyne is a regional city in Somalia. It was exciting news for me since I was missing my family. I thought, "Why don't I live with my family and continue my studies there?" So, I decided to move to Beledweyne.

One day, I saw one of my aunt's sons, who was in the Somali military. He told me that he was getting transferred to Beledweyne where my family moved to. I asked him if I could go with him. Then he said, "Ok."

I was delighted and thought; "Now I can live with my family!"

We travelled in a military lorry. The journey was in the night, so we arrived in the morning.

After two days of rest, I enrolled in a middle school and I was given a place in year seven. Since I was in a new school I had to make new friends. Even though all the students were Somalis, to them I was a new and unfamiliar boy. I tried my best to make friends. They asked me some questions about Mogadishu and my school there and why I moved to Beledweyne. They also tested me to find out if I was clever. In the end, most of them became my friends and they gave me a nickname, (Safar) The Traveller.

Chapter Two
Rural Development Adventure

It was the end of my year seven, when the Somali government decided to carry out a campaign in Somalia called **Ololaha Horumarinta Reer Miyiga.** A rural development campaign aimed to teach the Somali nomads how to read and write the Somali language. To view this, visit **Birth of the Somali Nation, YouTube.** A large number of students, teachers and other government employees like doctors, nurses were mobilised. The army and the police were also used where there was a need for security.

I was a member of a group sent to villages and nomads near the border of the Somali region of Hiiraan and Ethiopia. Our group went to a village called Defow near the border. The River Shabelle that follows from Ethiopia passes through Defow to Somalia.

Most of the inhabitants were farmers, and relied on the seasonal rainfall, so they weren't earning enough for their living. Some were nomads, who owned camels, cattle, and goats. The animal herders were poor too because their animals were being moved from one area to another looking for grass and water.

We, as a group with a teaching mission, tried to settle in the village. The villagers were happy to see us in their village because they had heard that we were coming to teach them how to read and write their language; which was exciting. In the first month or so, we brought our food from the city since there were no shops in the village. We started our mission of teaching the villagers every afternoon when they came back from their work.

After that, the government came up with an idea, which was quite challenging. Each one of our group had to eat with a family in the village. This idea was to teach us how to live with the villagers, whose way of living was very different from ours in the city. In doing so, we had to pay the families the whole food allowance that the government was giving us. Each member of our group was allocated to a family in the village. In the beginning, it was really hard to adapt, because their level of living was one of the lowest we have ever seen or heard of. Even though the villagers were farmers and lived on the banks of the River Shabelle, they didn't have water pumping machines, so they relied on the rainfall to water their farms. In addition, lack of education was a strong factor that caused them to be poor. This was one of the reasons that made the government carry out the rural development campaign.

Personally, my experience regarding living with a family was quite unbearable. The family I was allocated to was really poor in the way they made their food. At that time we were in the holy month of Ramadan, the month when Muslims fast from dawn to dusk for 29 or 30 days. I remember one day, it was just before dawn when I was given some food by the family. It was made of barely cooked corn with its skin on. It was hard to chew. Since I was so hungry and wanted to fast for the rest of the day, I decided to eat it and chew it as hard as I could. I had to take sips of water to swallow it. Unfortunately, I couldn't finish what was in the bowl, so I drank a lot of water to fill up my stomach.

My colleagues were also complaining too, but there was no match to my case. Therefore, the situation made me think of how I could find an alternative family to be with for the rest of the campaign.

One day I heard terrible news which made me extremely sad and heartbroken. It was the death of my cousin (the eldest of my aunt's sons Ali). Ali was an exceptional and outstanding brother who knew and couldn't forget the help my father had given to my aunt bringing up her children. When my family came to Beledweyne they had nothing to support themselves with no skills or experience to work in the city. Ali was working in the hospital as a senior nurse. He had his own family to support. I can imagine his salary wasn't even enough for his family. After the arrival of my family, Ali decided to dedicate and give a whole half of his salary to my family. This shows how much appreciation he had for my father. There is a Somali saying **(Libaax nin ganay iyo nin galadayba og)** which can roughly be translated as follows: **A lion can differentiate who hurt him from who helped him.** After hearing the death of my beloved cousin, I wasn't able to stay at work. Then I immediately decided to go to Beledwyne without permission from my team leader. It was early in the evening, when I saw a man from the village who was going to the city with his donkey. Since there wasn't any transport and I had no money, I had no choice but to go with the man with the donkey. The city was nearly thirty KM away from the village. We travelled through the whole night and reached Beledweyne in the morning. At home, I met my cousin's widow who was a very kind and considerate woman. She told me Ali died in Mogadishu not in Beledweyne. After a day of mourning and sorrow, I had to go back to work.

One day in the village, I met a young man who was looking after a herd of camels. We had some conversation, he told me how he liked learning how to read and write. I told him that I could teach him and his family. He was excited about the idea. For me, the idea seemed to be good because the camel's milk was something I wanted.

I said to myself, "I'll live with this family and still get on with my job teaching them how to read and write." I suggested that the young man needed to speak to his father and tell him the idea.

The next day, his father came to see me. He asked me if I was ready to go with their family moving from one area to another. I confirmed that it was OK with me. That way of life was better than the one I was in, because the nomadic life was familiar to me since I was born in the countryside. That was really a good chance for me to escape from the unbearable situation I was in. I told him that we needed to see my team leader to approve the deal. My team leader asked the man a few questions about my safety and told him they were going to take responsibility for looking after me.

The man assured my team leader that his family would look after me with great care. I felt really happy with the agreement. I packed my things, which were some books, pencils, some white chalk, and a small blackboard, that had a handle to hang it on a tree's trunk when teaching. The man helped me carry my things and off we went.

As I mentioned earlier, the nomads keep moving from one area to another, looking for pasture for their animals. The family had camels and goats. The camels were looked after by the young man and the goats were taken care of by the women. At that time, the family was based in an area, where their animals could find pasture and water.

In the morning, the animals were milked and the family had a good breakfast. The young man and I took the camels to the bushes, and the girls took the goats to the bushes for grazing. While the camels were busy grazing in the bushes, the young man and I would sit under the shade of a big tree and talk about how to read the Somali language. I started teaching him the alphabet and the sounds, which he enjoyed learning.

Occasionally, we would return home in the afternoon. I always tried not to miss those opportunities when I could catch up with the rest of the family to teach them as well. After the lesson, the animals were milked and the women cooked the supper. After having our meals, we all went to sleep. In the countryside, whilst sleeping we could hear the roar of lions as well as other wild animals. I was really lucky that I didn't see a lion or any other dangerous, wild animals during my time with that family.

The life of the nomads is adventurous and unpredictable. In the mornings, when we were taking the camels, we didn't know what to expect. Our everyday plan was to follow the camels wherever they go and to find pasture and water for them.

One day, the young man and I took the camels, as usual. Sometimes the camels would eat some leaves and soft tip of the branches from trees and then move on to find better trees. We kept following them. They moved further and further munching and enjoying their grazing.

It was midday when we decided to milk one of the camels and drank some milk. Milking the camels was one of my favourite experiences, which I had practised during my past days with the young man. After we had drunk the milk, we moved on to go further. The camels were enjoying their grazing which made us happy as well. Soon it became very late and we started to take our camels back to our area but we were nowhere near the area. It wasn't very long before the sun started to set.

The sky was covered with thick clouds, so it was getting darker and darker. We thought it was probably going to rain, but later we realised it wasn't going to rain in our area. It got even darker. We were in a thick forest where the trees were really bushy and very close to each other. It was hard to find our way among the trees. Sometimes, we ran into thorny trees that scratched our bodies and tore our clothes. With this problem, we had to keep looking after the camels.

Luckily, the camels knew the way back to our area, as camels normally know how to go back to their homes without a problem. We were doing our best to follow them. Sometimes there was lightning, so we had a glimpse of light around us and saw some trees and the camels in front of us.

After a very long and tiring day, we finally arrived home just after midnight. For me, it was a night that I had never imagined and certainly will never forget. It was an exhausting, difficult and unbearable experience. Unlike me, it was actually a part of the nomadic life for the people that I was living with, because they encountered this from time to time. This fact was quite obvious, because my friend, the young camel man didn't speak about that torturous night.

Days, weeks passed by, spending my time with them in the daily routine of the nomadic life. For them, the only new part of their daily activities was learning how to read and write their language. They liked it and found it fun.

Normally, when nomads hear that it has rained in an area they move to that area.

One day, they heard that it rained in an area that was not very far from where we were. It was about one day's trip away.

In the next morning, after milking the animals, and having our breakfast, we were told to take the camels towards the area they decided to move to. One of the male camels was loaded with the portable hut and the family's belongings, together with the children who were unable to walk. The male camel was well trained and trusted to carry all these valuables and the children. When walking with this kind of load and similar things, like when the family needed to fetch water from the wells and rivers, the trained male camels carried the loads properly. Because of the training, these male camels behaved differently compared to when they were with the other camels grazing in the countryside. If you had carefully looked at the loaded camel, you could have seen how responsibly it walked with its load on.

My friend and I started our journey with the camels heading towards the rainy area. It took us nearly a day. When we were around the area, we were exhausted and the camels needed to eat and graze the green plants. The area was mountainous with valleys. The camels started to climb up a mountain with a gentle slope. There were very green trees, from which the camels loved to eat. Since the camels enjoyed so much staying there munching the branches we decided not to move them from there.

Soon it was sunset. We had no idea where the rest of the family had settled. As a result, we had to spend that night there on top of the mountain with our camels.

The night was dark with no moon in the sky. The breeze started to blow from time to time, increasing its speed gently. It wasn't very long before I started to feel a bit cold. My friend and I looked at each other feeling the cold air. I especially felt the cold because the young man was well prepared for this kind of situation. He brought a sheet with him to cover himself when sleeping or whenever he felt cold. Unfortunately, I didn't bring my blanket or my sheet with me, because I thought that we would get home in the night, but that wasn't the case. The breeze blew and blew on the top of the mountain. It wasn't very cold, but in the daytime, it was quite warm and sunny, which of course made our bodies warm. In the night, it turned to be a bit cold. I needed something to keep me warm or a shelter to save me from the ever-increasing cold air.

My friend slept under his sheet, while the camels sat down to rest for the night. I was extremely helpless feeling colder and colder. The wind blew and blew and I felt desperate. When the situation is like that, necessity makes you think faster and faster. All of a sudden, I had an idea. One big camel was sitting near me.

I thought, "Why don't I hide myself behind the big camel and use it as a shield from the blowing cold wind?" I hid myself behind it and it worked. Sleeping next to a big camel was something that scared me. I had no choice though, but to take the risk. Sometimes the big camel leaned on its side towards me and nearly hurt me. In the end, I survived and kept myself warm behind it. After a long night and uncomfortable at times, the next day dawned and the sun rose. Then, the cold wind ended.

Usually, we learn from our mistakes. The experience of that night taught me a lesson. Whenever I saw nomad men, they would carry their sleeping sheets on their shoulders. Before that night, I used to wonder, 'Why do they carry it every day, wherever they go?'

That time around, I had learned that the nomadic life was unpredictable which meant they never knew where they were going to sleep that night, so they had to have their sleeping sheet with them all the time.

That day was a glorious sunny day, as are most of the days in east Africa. In that season, it sometimes rained but not on that day in particular. We milked one of the camels and drank for our breakfast. The camel's milk is very nutritious, much better than any other food. It is also used to cure diseases like cancer. That is why most of the camel men are extremely healthy and strong. We moved the camels down the hill. The young camel man knew that we could find the family not far from where we were, so we didn't rush to find them. Instead, we let the camels graze until the afternoon.

Late that afternoon, we tried to find the family which was not as easy as we thought. It took us a few hours, but in the end, we found them. The family and their animals were fine, and we were not worried about them in the first place.

Also, they were not worried about us either, as the area was very peaceful.

After a few weeks, it was time for me to return to the village, where my colleagues and my team leader were working. This time, it was the second phase of the campaign. It was about counting the people and their animals. This was officially called census data collection. We were given a large number of forms. After a day or two of induction and training, we were divided into groups, and each group was sent to a village, a water well, or a riverbank, from where nomad people got their water for themselves and their animals.

Like I mentioned earlier, the nomadic people in Somalia keep moving from one area to another so if you want to see them, you have to wait for them where they come for their water. We stayed and waited for them at their water sources. We counted those who came to us and their animals for a month. In the end, our plan was implemented. So we were adamant that we had collected almost all the data needed for the census data collection campaign.

The two phases of the campaign took place in every part of Somalia. I was really glad and still am to be part of that invaluable campaign for my country. After we had completed the big task, it was time for us to go back to the city.

After a few months or so, the census for Somalia was officially published. The percentage of the population who could read and write was seventy percent and the United Nations gave an award to Somalia for that reason.

When I arrived in the city, I found out that my family had moved to Mogadishu, the capital of Somalia. I stayed with some distant relatives for a few days and then travelled to Mogadishu to join my family. The journey took one day on the road because of the long distance between Beledweyne and Mogadishu. The other reason for the delay was that the road was rough. So the coach couldn't go any faster.

I arrived in Mogadishu late in the afternoon. Luckily, I knew how I could find my family because my relatives lived in the city. I went to a relative's house then they told me where my family was. After finding my family in the suburb of Mogadishu, I thought about the situation that my family was in. My family was new to the city facing all the odds. Imagine a nomadic family who came from the countryside two years ago, to a city that was very new to them and moving again to another even bigger city, with no skills or profession to earn living. My family's situation was really hard to manage.

With that in mind, my mission was to work as hard as possible on my studies. There was a hope that if I finished year eight with high marks, I could get some work training. With that in consideration, I started year eight with a genuine enthusiasm and an absolute determination to get high marks in every subject at the end of the school year.

Since our house had no electricity, some of my classmates and I used to go to the city parks, where there were lots of lights, to study and help each other revising our lessons. Libraries did not exist in Mogadishu at that time.

In the morning, our school was attended by intermediate-level students. I was in the final year of the intermediate level, year eight. We used to finish at noon. Then the primary level pupils used to come in immediately after us. I remember when we were approaching the last term of year eight; there was a teacher shortage at the primary school. For this reason, our headteacher came to our class and chose a few students in our year group to assist the primary school as volunteer assistants for the teaching staff in the afternoon and I was one of them.

The headteacher took us to his office and asked us to volunteer to help the primary school teachers in the afternoon. We were all happy to do so and started the work immediately. I remember teaching maths in year four primary school for a few hours each day after having lunch at home. Luckily, my house was not very far from my school.

Since I was studying my utmost and being a teaching assistant at my school in the afternoon, it wasn't long before it was time for our final examination.

After revising every subject and having numerous mock exams, most of us were undoubtedly ready to take part in the final examination with high hopes. After waiting patiently for the exam to begin we were given the timetable for the examination. We had two subjects a day over five days, so in total there were ten subjects.

After the examination, I kept thinking about it. In my opinion, for me most of the subjects in the exam were easy, and this was due to the hard work and the time I invested in my studies. So I hoped good results while I expected that I did exceptionally well in the some of the subjects.

After two months of a long wait, our examination results were released. To my delight, I passed all the subjects with good marks. As I hoped, I also had some very high marks.

My parents were proud of me. For my family, this was the beginning of a good hope.

Chapter Three
A Teacher's Adventure

Fifteen days after our results were released there was an announcement on Radio Mogadishu. The Ministry of Education wanted to recruit and train three thousand teachers for the primary and middle schools. I was not surprised by the news because I knew the teacher shortage in my school. Many of my classmates, who achieved high marks like I did, decided to go to high school and then university. Unfortunately, that wasn't an option for me, because of my family's financial circumstances. I was like a fruit that its farmer couldn't wait for it to fully ripen. I immediately decided to apply for the teacher training.

Two months later, there was an interview for all those who applied for the teacher training. I clearly remember my interview with a panel of senior officials from the Ministry of Education. They asked me two questions.

The first was: "Since you have very high marks, you are allowed to choose any type of high school. Why don't you continue your education?"

My answer was, "I need to start work."

The second question was, "Why do you want to be a teacher?"

My response was, "I would like to educate my people and also support my family."

All of a sudden, there was a sparkling smile on the faces of the interviewers, which gave me a clear signal of OK. One of the interviewers wrote OK on my job application letter which was on their table.

I went home with great hope and excitement. As I mentioned earlier, my family was struggling to make ends meet. So, while I was waiting to hear from the education authorities, I was helping my family to earn living in one way or another.

Finally, there was an announcement on Radio Mogadishu. It was about the commencement of the teacher's training. We had to go to a military training camp because that was the only place which was big enough to accommodate three thousand young teacher trainees.

The camp is called HALANE military training camp. It is located at the seaside near the Aden Abdulle Osman International Airport of Mogadishu. On our arrival day, we gathered in front of the camp's gate.

Imagine three thousand young men and women lined up in front of a military camp. We came from all over the country. They didn't let us go into the camp on arrival, but they made us line up and wait until almost everybody was there. Soldiers and their commanders came out of the camp and met us at the gate. They had battery-powered loudspeakers. They told us from that time onwards, we were expected to behave like military soldiers. That didn't mean that we were not being trained as teachers, but we were going to be managed by the military trainers. Furthermore, we were told that we were also going to be trained as soldiers to defend our country if need be. No wonder, because the country was ruled by a military government. At last, we went into the camp marching in our lines.

The young women were allocated to a separate part of the camp, whereas we were taken to another part of the camp. We settled in massive halls full of bunk beds. Each hall could fit at least one hundred and fifty people. After settling in those halls, our commander blew his whistle which meant "Come out quickly."

When we came out, we were told to line up. Nearly a hundred of us made ten parallel lines. Each one was around ten people. Our names were written in a register then we were told that we were going to be together for the rest of the training time. We were taken to a nearby seaside in the camp. We were told that trainee soldiers shouldn't have bushy hair. For that reason, we were given some razor blades to shave our hair. Since there weren't enough barbers to shave for nearly two thousand men, we were told to work in pairs shaving our hair for one another.

That work took a few hours to be completed. After that, we lined up and went to the uniform stores. We were given some uniforms, which were two sets of uniforms for each one of us. Immediately after that, we were told to go to our halls, change and come back as soon as possible. In no longer than half an hour, everybody was there in their line. Looking out in the camp the atmosphere had changed. Everywhere you look there were massive lines of uniformed personnel. We were told to sit down on the ground. Our commanders had to give us lectures about military discipline. They were talking about soldier's behaviour and how they respect each other's ranks. After that, we were taken to a massive hall where we had our lunch.

After two hours of rest, our commander blew his whistle for us to come out and line up. We were told how our timetable was going to be for the military training and the teacher training. The timetable would start early in the morning, just after dawn every day except on Fridays. We would line up and start jogging and marching in a big field on the seaside until sunrise. That was called the PE session. That was followed by breakfast, which would take about an hour. Thereafter we would get ready for our teacher training classes.

There we started the training that led us to be the great team of teachers for the nation. It was January 1976. After going into our classes, we realised that the authorities had chosen the best lecturers they could find from all over the country. They told us that the training would last for a year. That meant the course was an intensive course for a fully trained school teacher. That was why they brought the highly experienced lecturers for us. There were some foreign lecturers too. Of course, we were studying all the subjects, including English, Arabic, geography, history, biology, chemistry, physics, religion, education, and maths. The Somali literature and socialist studies were also included. This was the year the Somali Socialist Party was established.

On the other hand, we were being trained as soldiers, building our skills of tolerating hard life and difficult circumstances. The military personnel who were training us were really tough on us. They never tolerated any misbehaviours or misconducts. The whole week was a very busy time except on Fridays when we could relax. Those who, were from Mogadishu and around it could go out and visit their families and those who were from other regions could go to the city and come back to the camp at any time in the day.

Since I was from Mogadishu, it was a good opportunity for me to visit my family and see how they were doing and tell them how things were going in my training.

On Saturday, it was business as usual. In the first few weeks, the military training seemed to be hard for us before we got used to it. The soldiers found us quite weak and unprepared for the training. There were some complaints from us; however, the soldiers were relentless for their mission was to make us just like them. Soldiers were supposed to be tough, who never minded to be in any hardship that came before them. Our academic work in the camp had intensified too. We had to complete the teacher training in a very short time. After realising the tough tasks that we were facing, we had tightened our belts and faced them with bravery. After many months of hard work, I remember one Friday night we were allowed to watch a concert by a Somali national band called Waberi. It was entertaining and helped us relax for a few hours. Some of them were comedians who made us laugh while others were singers who sang really sweet songs. The music was nice and fun too.

As time passed we were getting used to the hard work. Most of the time we were almost ready before the morning whistle went off. Our morning P.E. exercise didn't seem difficult anymore. We were marching just like the commandos. We were greeting the high-ranked commanders with military salutes. Our complaints got less and less. Our academic work got better and better. We had some exams and almost every one of us did very well. There were some occasions when we were taken to some schools in Mogadishu for us to practise teaching. It was a good experience for us.

The end of our training came closer and closer. Some of the education authorities came to see how we were doing. Some military commanders came from the ministry of defence to watch us while marching and they were impressed and clapped when we passed near them. In October 1976, we participated in the 6th anniversary of the military revolution celebration on 21 October. We marched like military soldiers showing off what we had practised in our military training.

After that, we were told that it was the end of our teacher training. Therefore we were ready to start work.

After a few days of the celebration, we were informed that we were allocated to go to different regions of the country, where we would start working.

One day before our departure we received our first salaries. To me, it was a happy day. I was allocated to go and work in the Lower Shabelle region. A District called Sablalle. When I received my salary, I went to my family and broke the news to them. I gave them most of my salary. Since my family had no permanent income, I promised them that I was going to send them some money every month.

My parents wished me all the best and asked Allah to help me. I could see from their faces that it was a big relief for them. That was what I wanted to achieve ever since I started my learning journey. Help myself, help my family and help my people. In general, my motto was and still is to always be helpful and Allah will definitely help me. "All my dreams were going to come true," I thought. Then I returned to the camp.

The next day was the day of our departure. We were given some military vehicles or Lorries to take us to our destinations to start work. Our journey to Sablalle started in the morning. The road was tarmac for about thirty kilometres. After that, it was rough. Luckily, it wasn't a rainy season. Therefore, the road wasn't muddy. The weather was nice and sunny as always in east Africa. On our way, we saw so many people looking after their animals and some were working on their farms. In some areas, we saw fruit farms like mango, oranges but most of the farms were banana farms which were beautiful to see. Lower Shabelle used to produce the best bananas in the world, which were exported to Italy and then from there to the rest of the world.

While on our journey, we sometimes went into a sandy road which made our journey an uneasy one. However, our military lorry was able to take the challenge for it was a six-wheel-drive vehicle. So, we didn't stop for any difficulty we faced. While in the lorry, we kept ourselves busy talking about what we could see and telling one another some relevant stories.

We finally reached our destination two and half hours before the sunset. We were warmly welcomed by the people in the town. Our accommodations were shown to us. The town wasn't an old one. It was settled by people who were displaced by drought. The people used to live in the north and central Somalia. In those areas, it had not rained for two years. Then the government decided to move them to farmlands with a river, where they could have a good opportunity to start a new life. This is where the River Shabelle goes through. The Lower Shabelle region is one of the most prosperous regions of Somalia with vast farmlands and is extremely fertile. One can grow anything that can be grown in the tropical zones of the world. In addition to that, the region has a coastline along the farmland that is very near to it. The coastal area is sandy and sunny with no cold weather all year round.

Back to our arrival at the town, we were exhausted and needed some rest and food. The government was responsible for the provision of food and housing for both the new inhabitants and the government employees. They showed us a massive hall built for the government employees to dine and hold meetings in it. After we had our meal in the hall, they took us to our housing compound. The houses were made of very cheap local building materials and unsophisticated building methods were used. However, because of the pleasant weather we have in east Africa, the houses were just right and comfortable for us to live in. We had a very nice and comfortable sleep during the night with no disruptions at all. The next morning, after having our breakfast at the big hall, we had a meeting with the town's education authority in the big hall.

There were six schools in the town. Each one of us was allocated to a school. We visited the schools. They were not far from the town centre. The school that I was allocated to was called Iftin, which meant Light. The name was implying the light of the knowledge. Just like we say ignorance is darkness, while knowledge is light. Our first day in school was interesting. The school had twelve classrooms full of pupils. In each class, there were 35–40 pupils. There were two shifts, one in the morning and one in the afternoon. The morning classes used to start at seven o'clock and ended at noon, whereas the afternoon shift started immediately after noon and ended at five o'clock.

The people who lived in the town used to be nomads, who were stricken by droughts. They had no skills other than looking after their animals. Once they were settled in the farmland, there was a good plan for them set by the government to become farmers. They were being trained to do different jobs on the farms. Most of the adults helped to do the manual jobs on the farms, while others were trained as technicians like mechanics, machine operators, and also drivers.

All the children had to go to school, which was compulsory until they reached adult age. The school children loved learning. Since they were from the countryside and never saw the urban life, they liked going to school and learning new things. When the teachers taught them in their classes, they always listened with great interest and followed all instructions without hesitation. It was very rare to see some of them talking to each other while their teacher was teaching.

When they were out of school and saw their teacher in town, they ran to him and hugged him like their parents, who were absent from home for a long time. That showed the love and respect that they had for their teachers.

I remember one day, when I was teaching a lesson. I accidentally used an English word to explain something. One of the pupils put his hand up and asked me what I meant by the English word. I had to apologise and tell him what it meant. That showed how interested they were in their learning. By the way, we were not teaching the English language, instead, all subjects were taught in Somali.

Our first year of work had ended with success and a great experience. After two months of school holiday, it was back to work as usual. We started work with enthusiasm. One day, it started to rain heavily. The town's houses were very poor in quality. The houses were mostly huts made of branches from trees, and the roof was made of dried grass. Many families' huts were damaged by the heavy rain and needed help. We had no choice, but to start helping them. I remember when I chose some strong boys from the school and took them to the nearby countryside. We collected some long grass to help repair the family's huts. Since it was a rainy season, the families had the same house problems reoccurring, but we were all united to solve the problems that arose and succeeded to overcome.

A Few months passed into my second year in the school. One day, the headteacher called me into his office and asked me if I was willing to be his deputy headteacher. I wasn't fully convinced with the offer because many teachers in the school were much more experienced than I was. So, I thanked him for the offer and mentioned that I didn't have enough experience for the position. He confirmed that I was right, but he liked my honesty and the hard work I was doing. He added that he was going to give me some time to train me for the position. Since I was passionate about working hard, I could not resist the offer anymore and had to accept it.

The next day, we, the teachers, and our headteacher had a meeting in the office. The headteacher announced that from that day on, I was going to be his deputy headteacher.

As he promised the headteacher spoke to me regarding management and leadership. It was a good opportunity for me to get that training, which helped me to perform well in fulfilling my duties. Of course, I had my teaching timetable, while helping the headteacher do his work.

The teachers were really helpful except a few who seemed unhappy about my promotion. The teachers were told to inform me if they encountered any problems when the headteacher was busy. Apart from school work, we had other duties which were helping the people in the town to increase their urban life knowledge. There were some gathering occasions in the evening, in which people were attending to listen to some teachers' lectures. The people were asking about anything they didn't understand about the new life in the town because they were used to a nomadic life in the countryside.

In the middle of 1977, there was a war between Somalia and Ethiopia. The war was caused by a region controlled by Ethiopia but belongs to the Somalis. Once the war started, most of the Somali military was at war. In our town, the authorities announced that strong men were needed in the war. Most of the men in the town were called to be trained for the war. The teachers and the other government employees were not included. The town's men were put in groups and trained for a few weeks. Then they were sent to the battlefields at the border of Somalia and Ethiopia. In the town, everybody was listening to the radio to find out about the war. Within the first two weeks, we heard that the Somali army was advancing into the Somali region of Ethiopia. The people in the town cheered whenever they heard that kind of news. On the radio, there were songs of encouragement for the advancing Somali army. People loved those songs. They chanted and sang in the streets of the town.

Two months passed, the war was well into Ethiopia's territory and a large part of the Somali region was captured by the Somali Liberation Army. The third month into the war, we heard that many hundreds of Ethiopian soldiers were captured in the war and brought to Southern Somalia where we were. A few months later, we heard that the war was devastating for the Ethiopians, so it was inevitable for them to seek desperately needed help from the Soviet Union, who was a friend of both Ethiopia and Somalia.

To interfere in the war the Soviet Union had to choose one side and fight the other. To the dismay of the Somali people, The Soviets chose to side with the Ethiopians and decided to bring their military might to the war fields and bush the Somali army back to the Somali border with Ethiopia. Finally, they brought the war to an end.

In the town, people were taught how to read and write their Somali language. In addition to that, some of the teachers who had good Islamic knowledge taught the people about their Islamic faith, which they appreciated a lot. Those teachings helped the people to be good Muslims. Those Islamic teachings took place in the evenings, after the Maghreb prayers. I remember I was a very close friend to some of those teachers who were teaching the Islamic lessons. I used to go with them helping the people and the teacher when they needed me. That helped me increase my Islamic knowledge too, revising what I already knew and learning anything that was new to me. It is always wise to keep increasing your knowledge to help you be successful in this life and hereafter.

I remember one night, when it was raining, while we were asleep. We heard a knock on our door. I opened the door and there I saw policemen. They asked for the names of a few teachers. They were the names of my fellow teachers who taught the Islamic lessons at the town's mosque. They were taken into custody. The policemen didn't tell us anything. In the morning, we found out that few more teachers were arrested by the police, who were also other Islamic teachers in the town. We went to the police station and they told us that the teachers were taken away immediately after the arrest. In those days, the government was a pro-soviet socialist government, which was against anyone who taught Islamic teachings. The teachers were suspected to be against the socialist government. As I was a very close friend of some of them, I didn't hear them mentioning anything about the socialist system, nor anything about the government. They were only teaching the basic Islamic beliefs and the peaceful Islamic principles.

All of the teachers and other people were understandably horrified by the news. We further inquired about them and we were told that the National Security Services took them to an unknown location. Later in that week some teachers including me were called by the National Security Services in the town. They asked me about those teachers who were arrested. They asked me about what they were doing in the evenings at the mosque. I told them that they were teaching the basic Islamic practice like prayers, fasting, and all the relevant worshipping rules of Islam. Unfortunately, we did not hear of them until years later, when they were released.

Back to the school, one or two months passed when one day, some school inspectors from the Ministry of Education came into our school unexpectedly. Our headteacher was not at work that week, so I was in charge. When the inspectors came in, they told me who they were and what they wanted to do. As always, I was doing my job in the way my headteacher instructed me. So, everything was in place and the classes were running as usual. Because of that, I had full confidence. I told them the number of pupils in the school, the number of teachers and the number of classrooms. Then I answered all the questions they asked. After that, I took them to the classrooms, introduced them to the class teachers. The inspectors asked the teachers to show their lesson plans for the day. Luckily, I had already made sure that I had checked every teacher's lesson plan before they went into the classes and also signed and dated with my stamp on. The inspectors listened and looked at how the lessons were going on. They asked some pupils to find out how they understood the lessons.

The inspectors and I went back to the office. They told me to come to the meeting hall with all the teachers after we had released the pupils for lunch. After a few hours, it was time to dismiss the classes. Then we went to the meeting hall. The hall was full of teachers and their headteachers. The head of the education office in the town and the inspectors were sitting in front of us. The head of the education office welcomed the inspectors and thanked them for coming to see what we were doing. After that, the inspectors talked about their duties and what they wanted the schools do. They praised the effort of the town's education system and the hard work that most of us were doing. After that, they talked about the schools and said they were doing fine, but they said one school was outstanding and that was my school IFTIN. Then they called my name. Remember my headteacher was not at work that week. All the other five school headteachers were there. Everybody was surprised by the news. The crowd started to cheer and applauded. Even though I always liked to work hard, the recognition boosted my morale. So, I started to do my job with more confidence and enthusiasm.

A few days later, my headteacher came back to work. I told him about the inspection and what the inspectors had to say about our school. He was pleased to hear the news. From that day on, he relied on me more than ever before.

One day at school, it was break time, when a young girl who was in the final year of the primary approached me. She told me that her teacher asked her to meet him privately and that she refused to do so. It was strange to hear. She said, "The teacher threatened me if I didn't meet him." I asked her what she thought about what he wanted. She said, " I am not sure but I don't want to meet him anyway." In my view, the girl was old enough and mature to get married. In those days, the Somali Education system allowed children of any age to start primary school if they were not adults. To make sure that I was not against the teacher's idea without a good reason, I asked the girl "What about if he wants to marry you?" She said, "That is not good for me because teachers come and go to work somewhere else. So, I don't want to marry someone who is going to leave me here." I asked her how he threatened her. She said, " He said to me, I will make sure you fail in your examination if you don't meet me." I assured her that it would not happen and all she needed was to work hard for her upcoming examination. She was really pleased with what I said and told me that she would do so. I informed the headteacher what the girl told me. He wrote some notes in his book about the matter.

A Few months passed, and soon it was examination time. One day, when all classes were busy doing their examination. I was supervising the whole school going around the classes. All of a sudden, I saw the girl that the teacher threatened coming out of her class. She came to me crying. I asked her what had happened. She said, "The teacher has sent me out and he has taken my exam paper." To me that was unbelievable, but since I had heard the story before, it seemed to be true. I decided not to deal with it, but to pass it on to the headteacher who was sitting in his office. I was glad that I had told him before, so it wasn't new to him either. I told the girl to wait for me outside the office. I told the headteacher and he remembered it with anger on his face. He let the girl come into the office and went to her class then he called the teacher. The headteacher asked him a few questions and decided to send him to the town's education main office. The headteacher told me to go to the girl's class. Then the girl came back to the class to do her exam. Later, he met the teacher in the town's education office. Then a decision was made for the teacher to be transferred to another school.

After the end of the examination, it was nearly the end of the school year. It took us about two weeks to release the results. Soon, it was the beginning of two months of our school holiday. All the teachers packed up to go for their holiday. They were excited, longing to see their families. I was getting ready to go to Mogadishu, to have time with my family, but I had another task to do after going to Mogadishu. Two of my colleagues who were arrested that night by the police left their belongings with me and asked me to take their things to their families in Mogadishu.

Fortunately, it was easy for me to find the families and I gave them the things. I also broke the news to them about their sons. For the families, the news was devastating and heart-breaking. It was really sad to see the members of my colleagues' families breaking into tears after the news. By the way, in those days there were no telephone systems In most parts of the country. For that reason, the families couldn't get the news before I came to them. What was quite incomprehensible was that the young teachers who were arrested were doing their national service year after finishing their high school, before they went to university. They were unlawfully arrested without any charges and kept in jail. The government was a military socialist government. My colleagues' families didn't know what to do to help their sons. They had no clue as to where to find them. The only way that was coming into their minds was to find someone in the military, who was a highly ranked commander, and ask him to find their sons. Even if they found one, that would not guarantee a release for their sons, but only to see them. I used to see the families just to find out how the matter was going. They finally found their sons in a prison that was far from Mogadishu. That prison was in another region of Somalia. It was good news that they were in good health, but unfortunately, they were not allowed to see a judge or a lawyer to look at their case.

While I was on that school holiday, I saw some of my colleagues in the city. They told me that they had been to the

Ministry of Education and found out that some deputy headteachers were promoted to be headteachers. To my delight, they told me that my name was on the list of the newly promoted headteachers. Immediately after the good news, I rushed to the Ministry of Education to see the list of the newly promoted headteachers. Since it was not very far from where I was, Soon, I reached the Ministry of Education. The display board was outside the building of the Ministry of Education. I had a look at the list. Then, I found my name in it. It was great news for me. My hard work and the effort I made were recognised and my status was raised. "Now I can serve my country, helping my people while I am in a better position to make decisions at a headteacher's level," I thought. I came home and broke the news to my family. My parents were really happy to hear the news and appreciated that I was doing a good job. It was quite clear to my parents that my hard work was approved and the government promoted me.

After three weeks or so, it was time for me to go to work. I went to our regional headquarters office in Marka, the capital city of the Lower Shabelle region. I met the head of the Education Office. Since I had never been to the office before that day, I told him who I was. He welcomed me with great respect and congratulated me for the promotion. He acknowledged the hard work that we did in Sablalle and the role that teachers like me took in those years. I thanked him for the recognition and the appreciation he had shown. In our meeting, he told me that as a headteacher, I was allocated to work in a school in a farming village in the region. The village wasn't very far from the region's capital city Marka. The capital city is on the Indian Ocean coastline and the village was about twenty-five kilometres away from the capital city.

After the meeting, I was told where the village was. I stayed in a hotel for the night. In the next morning, I went to the village. Of course, no one knew me in the village, so I introduced myself to some elders. They were quite pleased to meet me. They showed me the school. It was quite small compared to the school I used to work in Sablalle. When I looked around the village, it was quite clear that they were all farm workers. I saw many of them carrying their farming manual tools like hoes, axes, and machetes. Their clothes were very rough and dirty. The houses were huts made of branches and the roofs were made of dried grass. Some children were running and playing in groups. I saw women carrying pots made of clay on their heads, which were filled with water fetched from a nearby river. There were few small shops from where people bought their food.

I asked the elders to find a house for me in the village. There was a house that could accommodate two persons. I decided to rent it. I went back to the school and asked the elders to get me some people to help me clean the school and get ready for the new school year. While cleaning the school, they told me that there had never been a headteacher in the school. They used to have some teachers in their school. I told them that their school would be much better than it used to be once they had a headteacher. Later that day, I was shown where the farms were and what they were growing. The farms were owned by an Italian company. They mostly grew bananas and some other fruits such as watermelon and oranges.

As I stated the villagers were all traditional farm workers for all their life in generations after generations. The Somali government wanted to improve their way of life for the better. The plan was to start educating them. Priority was given to the children to be educated, and then the adults. The school was already running, but what it needed was an efficient management system.

The adult programme was due to be started. They needed to learn how to read and write their Somali language. After that they could start learning other skills. My mission was to implement that plan. After settling in the village, I had a meeting with the elders and the parents of the school children. I explained how we wanted to help them to improve their livelihood. We pointed out that the plan was mainly to teach their children and the young adults at school. So they could have a better future. Also, the adults would have a good opportunity to learn how to read and write. They also had some other progressive programmes to benefit from.

Sadly, the planned programmes didn't go down to the villager's minds easily. This misunderstanding was uncovered when some strong boys and girls decided not to attend the school but instead, they went to work on the farms. Furthermore, many adults didn't come for the adult classes in the afternoon to learn reading and writing. For the school children, education was compulsory. Therefore, we could enforce the children's attendance at school. Disappointingly, we could not enforce the adult's attendance. Alternatively, we had to try and persuade them to come and learn for their own benefit. Since we were more than sure that it was highly beneficial for them, we didn't stop persuading them. Eventually, most of them accepted the idea and started to learn how to read and write the Somali language.

There was a radio programme that taught the villagers about some life skills; such as general health issues, cleanliness, and looking after their environment. Security and helping the police were also included. In general, the radio programmes were about learning good life skills and avoiding all bad habits.

The school work was going as usual. Since I had good school managing experience, my plans were all in place. Some of the teachers lived in the village while others were commuting from nearby towns. The pupils were not as enthusiastic as the pupils I used to teach in Sablalle. These pupils' learning performance depended on how the teachers' class management was. If they were strict, the pupils would work hard and if the teachers were lenient they wouldn't do much work.

After about six months of my first year working in the village's school and helping the villagers, I noticed that there was a conflict of interest that was going on. The Italian company who owned the farms wanted the people of the village to work for them, whenever the company needed and as many people as possible. The strong school children were not an exception. The adults were called even in the middle of the night without prior notice, let alone in the daytime. On the other hand, we, the education team, had a timetable for the adult learners. Disappointingly, most of the time, there were clashes of our timetable and the timeless farm work that the Italian company demanded from the villagers. The villagers had to choose whether to go to work or to come for their lessons. When the workers had to go to work, they informed their team leaders that they had a class to attend learning how to read and write the Somali language but missed it. They also showed their concern about the unexpected call for work.

The Italian company heard about the compulsory schooling for the children that caused the strong boys and girls not to come to work. This was a big cause of concern for the company. Everything was alright for the company before I came to the village. There was a Somali man who was working for the company. His position was the deputy manager of the company in the village. One day, that man and I met in the village. After some conversation with him, he invited me to dine with him in his house. He added that I could bring some of my teaching staff with me. The man and his family lived in a big house next to the Italian company's manager's house. The Italian man's house was big and modern. They both had electricity in their houses, whereas the villagers and the school didn't. The Somali and the Italian men had their own cars. I had heard that the villagers were paid very low wages and sometimes none, but instead, they were allowed to eat fruits and take some for their families. I was also told that the workers were given some plots of land to grow crops for their food. All these plans were in favour of the Italian company.

The invitation day to dine with the deputy manager of the Italian company came around. When it was time, I went to his house and with me was a teacher who was available at the time. He welcomed us in a very nice dining room. We had some interesting conversations without going into serious topics. Our conversation was mainly getting to know each other's backgrounds. The dinner was served. It was nice. Most of it was of course the type of which we could not afford to buy daily. After enjoying the meal, we came out of the house. His house had a garden with some parking spaces, where his car was parked. He invited both of us to come with him for a drive around the villages, where we didn't have a chance to visit before. I asked him if he was sure about it. He assured me it was alright. We accepted it and off we went with him.

After fifteen or twenty minutes of driving, we reached a village that was a bit bigger than ours. He drove the car off the road going into the village. He stopped the car and asked us to come with him. He told us that he wanted to see some people who lived in that village. He knocked on a door and someone opened it and welcomed us. We were taken to a room where other people were already sitting. He knew the people as they shook hands with him happily. He introduced us to the people and then we sat with them. It was a big room, enough for many people to meet.

After a little while, somebody from the house brought in some green leaves called khat. I recognised the green leaves because they were famous leaves chewed by some Somali people. I knew that it was a stimulant drug-like and addictive. Our driver received the bundle of the khat and distributed it to every one of us. I was not happy at all, because I hated using it. Others were happy to chew it. My fellow teacher who was sitting next to me was happy to chew it. I decided not to say anything but to pass my share of the khat to my colleague. There were some flasks of tea used by the men to sip with the khat. I poured the tea into a cup and started to sip.

After a little while, our driver decided for us to go. We went into the car and he drove us back to our village. While on our way, he asked me whether I liked chewing khat. I told him that I didn't. He said, "It is really good for people to sit together and have good conversation while enjoying chewing it."

I told him that it was bad for health and addictive too. I added that it would also cause a real financial problem.

He smiled and said, "I can help you pay for it."

I said, "Thank you but that is only a temporary offer, once I get addicted to it, it is me to go and buy it."

He said, "If you can't afford it there will always be some good people to sit with."

We reached our village before we came to a conclusion of our conversation and we had to leave it there.

When I came home, I started to think of what the man was trying to do. Why did he invite me for dinner? Why did he take me to that house and gave me the addictive khat? Why did he try to persuade me to chew the addictive khat? What would he benefit if I became a khat addict? All those questions needed answers. I started to think of the conflict of interest between the villagers' work for the Italian company and the new educational system that I came up with. I thought he was trying to make me his close friend, whom he could control his decisions when he wanted to. For example: in that case, he could tell me to let the people go to work for the company whether there was an education programme or not, including the strong school boys and girls.

Our first year of work in the village ended in mixed circumstances. On one hand, we made some progress, but on the other hand, our education plan didn't go smoothly. In the end, we had a good hope to do a much better job next year. We finalised our first year then went for our two-month school holiday. We came back with great interest and passion to do better this year. I went to the education head office of the region and brought some new textbooks for the school. I organised everything to plan. Both the school and the adult education programmes started well without any interruptions.

The family of the Somali man who was the deputy manager for the Italian company had some cattle kept in a cow house near my house. They used to sell the cows' milk to the villagers. I ordered a small bottle of milk every night. A young lady who was a sister-in-law of the deputy manager of the Italian company used to bring my bottle of milk to me and collected the payment. A month or so passed when one night the young lady brought my milk and told me that she could not read and write the Somali language. So, she wanted to learn how to read and write. I told her that we had an adult class in the afternoon.

She thought for a few seconds and said, "I am quite busy at that time." She added, "Can you teach me this time every night?"

I said, "That is impossible but there are some lady teachers whom I can ask to help you."

She said, "I will think about that."

From that night on, whenever she brought the milk she would flirt with me but I wasn't interested, because I knew my limits. It was quite clear, she was trying to attract me into a relationship, but what she didn't know was that I was the only one who was working for my family. For that reason, I couldn't have a relationship and get married. Since

I wasn't obliged to explain my situation, I just ignored her constant flirts.

Around a month or so passed, when one night I met the young lady and her mother in the village. The young lady told her mother who I was and said to me "This is my mother." To my surprise, the mother sounded like she had heard about me. After having some conversation about the school and the village, the mother ended our conversation with a suggestion. Saying, "You are a young man. If the government trusted you to run this school, we can trust you with our daughter too."

I just smiled at her and said, "Thank you."

Due to the war of 1977 between Somalia and Ethiopia, the Somali government's political situation started to deteriorate from time to time. There was an attempted military coup against the Somali government that was unsuccessful. As a result, the government started to arrest a lot of suspected people. Tensions were felt by some clans who thought they were targeted and started to be anti-government. The government's development projects were destructed and some were halted by the political crisis. The crisis affected the government's financial management. There was ever-deteriorating inflation. Inevitably living costs started to rise. The government couldn't solve the problem and didn't pay attention to the government employees' salaries. Consequently, there was corruption and bribery that swept across the government organisations. Some radio programmes were praising the leaders and how things were going but in real life, everything was getting worse. As I was one of those employees who were badly affected by the situation I had some conversation with the head of education in our region. He appeared to feel the same as me but he expressed it diplomatically.

My family in Mogadishu was having some unsolvable problems with the cost of living. Since our salaries were not increased to match the rising prices, my income was not enough to feed my family and me, let alone the other necessary expenses. I decided to write a letter to the Minister of Education asking him to transfer me to Mogadishu where I could live with my family, enabling us to live on my salary together or to let me resign from my work altogether.

Back to school, of course, I didn't show my political and financial feelings to my fellow teachers or anybody else but I got on with my job as usual. I tried my best to run the school to the end of the school year. We had no problems and everything went smoothly, until the end of the school year. We started our two-month school holiday. I was feeling nervous and looking forward to making a final decision about the letter I sent to the Minister of Education. I went to our regional office and asked him if there was a response from the Minister of Education about my letter. I was told that there was no letter addressed to me from the minister. Since it was a school holiday, I had the opportunity to go to Mogadishu. I decided to go and see the Minister of Education asking him to look at my letter and make a decision for me.

After I saw my family, I went to the Minister of Education in the morning. When I arrived at his reception, there was his secretary. I asked him if I could see the minister. He told me to take a seat at the reception. He went into the minister's office and came back within a few minutes. He told me that the minister was in a meeting so he couldn't see me straight away. I had to wait until the meeting had ended. After that, I was able to see the minister. I greeted him and introduced myself to him then I told him about my letter and asked him to make a decision. He told me that the government was against the idea of resignation. He advised me not to press for resignation or else they would arrest me. Regarding the transfer to Mogadishu, he made it clear that it was impossible, and if I insisted on the transfer I had to go and work in the northern regions of Somalia which was not an option for me at all.

To me, it was quite clear that the minister didn't pay any attention what so ever to my problem. He threatened me with arrest. Was I a criminal just because I asked for resignation? The transfer option he offered me was to deter me from thinking about it. I made it clear to him that my problem was a pure financial difficulty that made me come to him.

I said, "Thank you, I will make my own decision later."

I went home and thought about the matter long and hard. I decided to go to my regional head office and tell him about the meeting I had with the minister. The head of the regional education office was sympathetic about my problem and decided to transfer me to a town that was the nearest to Mogadishu that he controlled. That town is Afgooye which is around thirty kilometres away from Mogadishu. The transfer was very kind of him and that was the best he could do for me. I thanked him but unfortunately that couldn't solve my problem because it was impossible for me to live with my family and travel thirty kilometres every day back and forth. I came back to Mogadishu and made my final decision as to what to do next.

It seemed to me that the government was corrupt and didn't want to solve the country's financial and political problems. For those reasons, working for the government didn't hold my future aspirations, let alone my financial problems at that time. In the end, I finally decided to quit my job without resignation. That was the beginning of the year 1981, ten years before the collapse of Somali military government.

Chapter Four
Risk-Taking Adventure

I was trained as a teacher, then, worked in the Lower Shabelle region for five years. In the meantime, my family lived in Mogadishu. My brothers and sister went to school in Mogadishu and my mother started to sell things in the market. Our income was too little to cover our living cost. While this was our financial situation, I had to make the hard decision of quitting my job without resignation. As I mentioned before, the Somali military government didn't want their employees to leave their positions without the permission of the officials. I applied for resignation but the Minister of Education threatened me with jail. So leaving my job without official resignation was a real risk, but I was left with no option.

I thought about my future employment and how I could find a better job. At that time, there were no private schools in Mogadishu. I thought about working for foreign private companies in the country. I had heard their pay was much better than the government salary. I asked myself, "Do you speak different foreign languages to try and find a job from those companies?" The answer was no. Then I started to think of learning some foreign languages. While I kept thinking of that, I heard that the Italian Embassy had a department for the Italian culture, teaching some Somali people how to speak the Italian language. It was good news for me. I went there and enrolled. I started to attend for three afternoons every week.

After two months or so, I heard that the French Embassy was doing the same as the Italian Embassy, teaching the French language. It was another opportunity for me to learn another language. I went there and enrolled in a beginner's class. In Somalia, we had six working days and on Fridays, people were off work. I used to go to the Italian Embassy for three afternoons and went to the French Embassy in the other three afternoons.

After around four months of attending the Italian language class, I remember one afternoon, when the Italian teacher, who was a lady, was explaining a lesson said to us, "Do you understand the meaning of this word?"

The whole class went quiet. She repeated the question. Then I put my hand up. She pointed at me. I told her that I knew the meaning of the word. She asked me if I could tell her in English. By the way, the Italian teacher told us earlier that she spoke some more languages other than her own Italian language. I told her the meaning of the Italian word in English. She was pleased that she had someone in the class who could help her when she got stuck. She asked me to tell the rest of the class the meaning of the word in Somali. After doing what she told me to do, she asked me to sit in the front row to help her when there was a need. Then she said, "Sei il mio braccio desro." Which meant: you are my right hand. It was a real morale boost for me that made me concentrate on the language lessons and I spent more time studying.

In my French language class, there weren't any Somali people except me. All the other learners were foreigners who worked for the United Nations Office in Somalia. After the Somali-Ethiopian war in 1977, there were a huge number of refugees who came from Ethiopia to Somalia. The UN was helping the refugees.

The French language teacher spoke Italian but only a little. All the learners in the class spoke English.

One day, the French teacher wanted to tell us the meaning of a French word but no one in the class understood. The teacher got stuck and said I can only tell you in Italian. I put my hand up and asked him if he could tell me the word in Italian. He was really glad and asked me, "Do you speak Italian?"

I said, "A little." Then he asked me if I spoke English too.

I said, "Yes." he was delighted to hear that. Then he told me the French word in Italian. I told him that I understood it.

He said, "Do you know it in English?"

I said, "Yes."

He said, "Could you tell the class in English?" Then I told the class the meaning of the French word in English. The learners who were waiting and listening patiently to our conversation finally understood the meaning of the word and appreciated the help I provided. The teacher said *"c'est très aimable de votre part"* which meant "That's very nice of you."

In my opinion, learning how to read and write the French language is much more complicated than learning how to read and write the Italian language. So I had to pay more attention to the pronunciation and the spelling of the French words. After we spent three or four weeks in the French class, I was called to come to the office. The French course manager was sitting in the office. He spoke to me in French and asked me if I had paid for the fees. I responded to him in French and explained that I had some financial difficulties at that time, but I was going to pay soon. The manager was really impressed by the fact that I was able to express myself in French despite being in the French class for only a few weeks. He said, "Très bien vous pouvez aller en classe." Which meant: Very good you can go back to class.

After a while, the Italian-speaking French teacher was replaced by an English-speaking French teacher. This time our French was getting better than before. Our new teacher was pleased to see our understanding and started to tell us some French stories in French. Those embassies teaching their languages aimed to teach their culture to the respective country's people.

After around two years of learning the two languages, I was quite confident to go to any foreign company and ask for a job using the languages I spoke.

One day, I was told that there was an Italian company that was constructing a factory on the outskirts of Mogadishu. I went to them and they told me that there was a chance to get a job but I had to come back a week later. I came back on the day they told me to. There were so many people looking for jobs. The manager, whom I met a week before, and another man came out of their office. The manager saw me and spoke to the other man saying *"Questo uomo parla italiano, l'ho visto la settimana passato."* Which meant: This man speaks Italian, I saw him last week. The man was pleased to hear that and asked me my name. Since I hadn't resigned from the teaching job I used to do for the government, I had already planned to change my first name. I intended to get an experience letter that I could use for future employment. Also, the company didn't ask for an ID when recruiting Somali workers. The Italian man wrote my name. I was the first person to be recruited. The other people were asked if they had any skills. I interpreted for anyone who needed help. The Italian man didn't speak any other language, so he made me his assistant and interpreter. That meant I was the Italian team leader's right-hand man.

Most of the jobs they were doing were construction which was welding and fitting pipes. Most of the technicians were Italians and the helpers were Somalis, who didn't speak Italian. There were many groups of workers who were doing different jobs in the project. In our group, I was the only Somali man who spoke Italian, so all the Italians in our group who had Somali helpers relied on me to interpret. I also made sure all misunderstandings were resolved. The salaries were really good compared to the government salaries.

After I started my new job, my family's financial problems were solved. I even had some savings. After eight months of working for that company the contract came to an end. So we had to look for other jobs in the city.

Chapter Five
Arabian Desert Adventure

Whilst looking for a job, I had heard that one close friend of mine, who was my distant relative, got a visa and went to Kuwait. At that time, there was political crisis and uncertainty of employment in the country, so people were thinking about travelling abroad to find work. The government warned the embassies against issuing visas to Somali citizens. That restriction made it extremely difficult for people to find visas to travel abroad. I enquired about how my friend had found the visa and travelled to Kuwait. I was told that his uncle knew someone, who was working for the Kuwaiti embassy in Mogadishu and had helped him to get a visa.

That Uncle was my distant uncle too. I went to him and explained my situation then asked him to help me and a cousin of mine who wanted to travel. He told me to bring my passport and my cousin's passport to him. After a few weeks, my cousin and I received our visas to travel to Kuwait. It is a small country that is oil-rich in the Arabian Gulf States. Luckily, both of us had some money to buy tickets for the flight. Both of us had saved some money while working for the Italian company. We booked our flight to Kuwait.

Our departure date came and we went to the Mogadishu Airport. Since we had no heavy luggage we immediately preceded to the security checks and the immigration. In a very short time, we were in the waiting area. Later, we noticed some men, who were not travelling but looking at the passengers. My cousin, who was sitting next to me, was picked on by a man. Later, he told me that the man was a security serviceman, who knew him. The security serviceman wanted to catch government employees, who were trying to leave the country without resignation. My cousin worked as a teacher just like I did, and left his job without resignation. The security serviceman took my cousin to a corner and without delay my cousin promised the man some money for letting him go. The man agreed and my cousin showed him his brother who was standing outside the waiting area. My cousin's brother was there to see us off on our flight. My cousin's brother promised the man that he will pay him.

My cousin came back to me and soon the security serviceman was with us again, but this time it was my turn to be interrogated. He took me to a corner and asked me if I worked for the government as a teacher. My answer was, "No." Then I backed up my word with a letter of experience from the Italian company that I worked for. While the man was looking at the letter, the passengers were called to board the airplane.

Since the security serviceman had nothing to accuse me of, I said, "Sorry," and grabbed my letter from him and hurried to board the airplane. My cousin and I sat next to each other. Both of us were worried and anxious because of what happened in the waiting room. With all that in mind, we sat without even looking at each other. We were impatiently waiting for the plane to take off, because the security servicemen could come in the airplane at any time and picked on anyone they wanted. The other unbearable fact was that no one could tell who the security servicemen were. They normally wore plain clothes.

Every minute we waited for the plane to take off felt like an hour. In the end, nobody spoke to us and the airplane took off. After that, we felt a bit relieved but not fully, because we had heard before, on the Somali Airline planes there were undercover security service people. We were worried that talking to each other would cause us a problem. In addition to that, we never knew who was sitting next to us. We kept our mouths shut and pretended like we never knew each other.

After flying for two hours, a meal was served. Even though we never felt that we were out of danger, it was nice to have a meal on an airplane. We were flying away from our own country in which we never felt safe since we left our government jobs without resignation. All this was caused by the government who never authorised the resignation. After a long fearful flight, we finally landed at the airport of Abu-Dhabi. We got off the Somali Airplane and went to the transit area. Eventually, we were relieved and could speak to each other. Since it was our first time travelling abroad we enjoyed going around the duty-free shops. We saw some beautiful gifts, a variety of sweets and many types of delicious foods. We could not think of buying anything expensive. We bought the cheapest food we could find to wait for our next flight to Kuwait. We kept ourselves busy going here and there. Sometimes we sat on the seats at the transit area. The airport was impressively decorated and looked beautiful.

After four or five hours of waiting, it was time for our flight to Kuwait. That flight didn't take very long because the Emirates are not far from Kuwait. We landed in the Kuwait City Airport and headed to the arrivals. There were so many long queues of people from all over the world lined up for entry. My cousin and I joined the queue that seemed to be the shortest. The queue was moving very slowly. It took us around forty minutes to reach the immigration officer. When I gave my passport to the officer, he looked at the visa page suspiciously reading what was written on it. He looked at me and pulled a drawer from his desk. He got a small stamp and stamped cancel on my visa page. He showed me a handwritten date in Arabic numbers.

He said, "You have fiddled with the date and changed it."

He pointed to a waiting room and said, "Sit down there you are going back to your country."

I was shocked and said to myself, "Little does he know how hard it was to come out of my country." I sat down and thought for a while.

In my mind, I was imagining how bad it would be going back, after going through all the difficulties that I had experienced. I tried to calm myself down, but it took me a while to do so. In the end, I started to think about the writing on the passport pages, especially the visa page. I didn't write anything on the visa page or anywhere in the passport.

I asked myself, "How can I tell him that I didn't do what he said?" I stood up to approach him. He saw me coming and shouted at me saying, "Sit down there."

I wondered how cruel and badly behaved the policeman was!

I turned back and started to think again. I thought of a time when I had a good look at the visa page when I was at home in Mogadishu. Luckily, I remembered that there was a stamped date on the visa page, which was written in Latin numbers. The date he was talking about was written in Arabic.

I thought, "Now I can show him that Latin stamped date then he can change his mind."

I went to him and he saw me coming again. He was furious and nearly ordered for my arrest. I ran back to the waiting room feeling terrified and helpless. I started to think of how I could show him the evidence that I remembered. It was impossible for me to go to him on my own. Also, it was a bad idea to wait doing nothing. The policeman was a sergeant. I thought of the soldiers' hierarchy. I thought, "If I find a higher-ranked policeman in the airport, he might be able to speak to him." However, the question was, how could I find one? I couldn't go anywhere to find a policeman because I had to be there all the time.

After a long time, sitting there helplessly, I suddenly saw a police commander with stars on his shoulders. I stood up and hurried to him. I greeted him and started to speak to him in Arabic. But due to lack of practice, my Arabic was quite poor, so I asked him if he could speak English. To my surprise, he seemed happy to find someone who could speak

English with him. I told him my problem then I mentioned the stamped date on the visa page.

He said, "Don't worry you will be fine."

He went to the immigration policeman and got my passport from him. Then he came back to me. I showed him the stamped date which was lightly inked but visible. He took my passport back to the policeman and showed him the stamped date. I could imagine how embarrassing that was to the immigration policeman. The policeman stamped another cancel on his previous cancel stamp diagonally on my passport' visa page. Then, he stamped ENTRY with a one-month visit visa.

Just before I left the policeman's counter. There was a Somali man at the counter. The policeman asked him who he was visiting, but the Somali man didn't understand a word of the Arabic language. He was lucky that I was still there. He asked me to speak to the policeman.

I said, "What is the matter?" In Arabic; the policeman repeated the question to me. I looked at the Somali man and asked him who he was visiting.

He said, "My brother." Before I told the policeman, I remembered what was written on my visa page, which was a made-up host.

I said to the policeman, "Look, it is written on the page."

The immigration policeman started to stamp the entry visa on the Somali man's passport. We both went out of the entry area.

Unfortunately, my cousin was still in another long queue. Since I could see him in the distance, I called him to come near me. I asked him what was wrong. He showed me his disembarkation card on which the immigration officer wrote some Arabic words that I couldn't read due to the handwriting. My cousin said "The immigration officer wrote this and told me to go to another queue. Then, when I came to the other officer's counter he had a look at the disembarkation card and told me to go to another queue."

I immediately understood that they were joking and having a laugh with him. Luckily, when we were on the airplane to Kuwait I was helping many people to fill in their disembarkation cards. I had some unused cards left in my handbag. I pulled one out and filled it in with my cousin's details. I gave it to him, then, I took the previous card off him. He went into a new queue and after a long wait he got his entry visa stamped on.

Once my cousin came out, we had a look around, and there we saw two Somali men who were on our flight. I asked them if they knew where they were going or if anyone was coming to pick them up. They told us that no one was coming for them and also they didn't know where they were going. That was bad news because we were just like them. That meant all four of us didn't know where to go. We all looked at each other hoping that one of us would come up with an idea. I said, "Let us go out of the building we might find someone who happens to be a Somali." We came out and there was no sign of someone who seemed to be Somali. I looked around and saw some taxis waiting for passengers. I thought of the time, it was one o'clock in the morning. I thought of a hotel to stay in until the morning.

I told my fellow Somalis that I had an idea. I went to a taxi driver, and they followed me. I asked the driver if he could take us to a hotel. He agreed and drove us off. While driving, I asked him if he could take us to a cheap hotel.

He said, "I don't know about prices but I will take you to a hotel." He took us to an impressive hotel called Holiday Inn. When the taxi stopped in front of the hotel, there were two uniformed porters. They immediately took our bags to the reception. I was quite sure that the hotel was too expensive for us to stay in, because it looked splendid. We went to the reception having little hope of staying there.

The receptionist was an Arab man. He greeted us with an Islamic greeting. I responded to him with a salaam too. Since my Arabic wasn't good enough, I asked him if he spoke English.

He said, "Yes."

I asked if they had rooms available.

He asked me what kind of rooms we wanted.

I said, "The cheapest ones, we want to stay for the remaining hours until the morning."

He told me some prices that I was certain we were unable to pay. I shook my head showing our concern about the prices. While he was telling us the prices, a French-speaking man came from the back of the reception. The receptionist told the man that the prices were too much for us.

The Arab man asked us, "Are you students?"

I thought that there were some discounts for the students. Then I said, "Yes."

He looked at the French man and spoke French with him. I confirmed what he said, in French.

The Arab man asked me "Do you all speak languages?"

I said, "Yes."

They decided to reduce the prices to the lowest possible for us.

Unfortunately, even the lowest prices were beyond our reach. I thanked them for trying to help us. Then I confirmed that we couldn't afford it. They both agreed that they couldn't do anything about it. They called a taxi driver who was waiting for passengers outside the hotel and asked him to take us to the cheapest hotel in the city.

He took us and whilst driving he was talking on his radio. He was probably asking his control centre to ring cheap hotels. After going a very long way, he found a cheap hotel for us. They had one room with two single beds in it and a washroom. With all the difficulties we had in the night, we couldn't refuse and decided to stay in the room until the morning. Before we knew it, it was the morning. Then we left the hotel.

Even though none of us could think of where to go, to find our fellow Somalis, we all agreed to go on the streets. We walked for a while, looking around, hoping to find a Somali person. If we found one, at least they could help us find other Somali people who then would help us find the people we were looking for. Suddenly, I had an idea. I said, "Let us speak to a taxi driver and ask if he knows the Somali embassy." My friends agreed, and there we found a taxi.

He thought for a second and said, "Do you know the Somali flag?"

We said, "Of course."

He said, "I'll take you to the area where the embassies are, and you look for the Somali flag."

It seemed to be a good idea, so we agreed. He drove and drove, hoping to see our flag.

Finally, we saw a flag, but it was a German one.

He said, "Is that it?"

We said, "No."

He kept driving. Luckily, the next was the Somali flag. We were all delighted to see it and thought we were home.

We came into the embassy's reception room. There were some senior Somali gentlemen, sitting and talking to each other. They welcomed us and noticed that we were new arrivals from Somalia. We told them what we went through that night.

One of them said to his friends; "Stop asking them questions." And he asked one of the men to take us for breakfast and bring us back. There were in brotherly hands. That was what we were lacking last night. For your information, the people who helped us knew none of us. They were helping us only because we were their Somali brothers. That is a part of the Somali culture.

One of the men took us in his car to a restaurant, then, we had a very nice breakfast. Whilst having our breakfast, the man was telling us about his long experience while he had been living in Kuwait. He paid for our breakfast and soon he brought us back to the embassy, where the other men were waiting for us. They told us that the day was scheduled for the Somali people to come and get what they needed from the embassy. That meant people could meet there and have some conversation in the waiting room. They asked us some questions about our country. The questions were generally about the overall situation of Somalia. We told them that it was alright without going into details.

Since they knew we wanted to be taken to somewhere to rest, they asked us if we knew some people in Kuwait.

We said, "No."

In that case, the Somali people who live abroad have a system to welcome every Somali person who is new to that country. They asked us which tribe each one of us belonged to. That means every Somali person is a member of a tribe. So, their tribe will take care of him or her. Since many people were coming to the embassy, it didn't take us long to be taken care of. My cousin and I were taken by a man who was a member of our tribe.

The Somali people who live in the Arabian Gulf and the African countries have a system that works like a mini social welfare system. The people from a particular Somali clan, who lived and settled in a particular country, collected contributions from their members and used the money to help their people who were new arrivals and also if any major problem arose, that couldn't be solved except by collective effort.

Back to our story, my cousin and I were taken to a flat where many people were living. They welcomed us warmly. As we expected some of them were familiar to us. Of course, all of them were single males. If the new arrivals were families or single females, they would go to other flats. Later, we found out that the people we came to were mostly new to the country. Some had come from neighbouring Iraq that was at war with Iran. It was the end of 1983. The flat's rooms were overcrowded. However, since we were with our people whatever the circumstances were, we could call it 'Home'. From that day on, we started to enquire about how life was going and how we could survive in the country. What we found out wasn't favourable to us.

It was really hard to find a job in the country especially when you were unskilled. The other obstacle was; if you were living in the country illegally. We came as visitors but we intended to stay and look for jobs. That meant we were going to stay in the country illegally. Everybody in that group was trying to find a job. We started looking for work too. Since most of us were unskilled we were looking for any jobs that we could do. As a daily routine, we normally left home early in the morning and came back late in the afternoon. Different groups went to different areas and all came back with no luck of finding jobs.

After two months of our arrival in the country, I was told that there was a chance of work for those who were educated. Job seekers who could take part in an academic test were invited to apply. There were some vacant positions at a seaport in Kuwait. I went to the place where they held the test. Many people from many different nationalities were interested in the vacant positions. The test was quite easy for me. I handed in copies of my certificates and my job application form stating the languages I speak. Despite the large number of applicants, I had a good hope. But my real worry was my illegal stay in the country. After two weeks, the results of the test were released. Fortunately, my name was the third person on the list of those who got the jobs. My friends and I were thrilled with the news. There was a notice for those who succeeded in the test, saying they had to bring their documents within two weeks from that day.

Knowing that I was staying in the country illegally, I couldn't present my passport to the authorities. It was a good try but not a success. We kept looking for jobs walking through the sweltering heat of the Arabian Desert. Due to the unbearable heat, we were sipping mineral water to try and keep our bodies cool. Apart from the hot weather, sometimes there was dust that was falling from the sky like rain. It looked like a very thick fog. It made visibility impossible which made many vehicles collide.

Three months after my good try to find a job, but deterred by my illegal stay in the country, someone who had heard that I spoke French, came to our house. He told me that there was a French company, who was looking for someone, who spoke French and other languages. I asked him if he could show me where the company was. He promised me that he would show me. It was in the morning, when he took me to the company. He showed me the building where the company was. It was a tall building, so I went upstairs.

I was greeted by a French man, saying, "How can I help you?" I told him that I was looking for a job. He took me to an office where there were many desks and many employees. The man spoke to one of them and told him about me.

The man said to me, "Good morning," In French.

I responded, "Good morning," In his language.

He asked me if I spoke good French.

I said, "Yes, as you can understand."

He said, "Do you speak English?"

I said, "My English is better than my French."

He called a man who was in another office and told him about me and the languages I speak. The other man came out and asked me if I spoke Arabic as well.

I said, "Yes."

They both smiled and decided to give me an application form. They said, "Bring it tomorrow with your documents."

I took the application form and went home. This time the matter was much more serious than before. It was not try and see what happens. Life was getting harder and harder at home. None of our unemployed group found a job. I was the only one who had hoped to find a job because I was looking for both unskilled and skilled jobs that I was able to do. If I did find a job, it meant good support for our unemployed group who were struggling with the daily life.

I asked my friends their opinions about how we could make sure I didn't miss the opportunity. We all decided to think about it long and hard. In the end, we came up with an idea and agreed. The idea was to use a copy of a friend's residence visa. The friend was the same age as I was. I went to him and told him the plan to which he kindly agreed. He made a copy of his passport and gave it to me. I filled the application form using the details of my friend. I went to the French company and handed my job application form in. They looked at it and found out how many languages I speak. To them it was impressive.

There was a Lebanese man who spoke all the languages I speak. He tried to speak to me in Italian, but his Italian was very poor. He told me that he didn't practise it for a long time. The office was a local branch for the company, so they called a man to take me to the main office. We went into a massive compound which was the company's main office. He took me to their human resources manager.

He told me to wait outside the office and he went into the manager's office with my application form.

In a short time, he came to me and said, "Wait for the manager to call you in."

It wasn't long before the manager called me. I sat with him. He asked me how much salary I was expecting. I told him that my previous employer used to pay me two hundred and fifty Dinars per month, so I was expecting three hundred Dinars per month. He suggested that they would pay me two hundred and seventy-five dinars per month. Then I agreed. The manager signed the application form and gave it to me then he sent me to the next-door office to get my work ID card.

I went to the office and gave them my signed application form with a copy of my passport.

They had a look at the residence page then they said, "You need a permission letter to work for a company, you can get it from your sponsor." I went out of the office, then, I thought for a minute. I had no option but to go home. When I came home I saw some of my friends and told them what happened. We talked about why they asked for a letter of permission to work for a company. One of my friends said, "In this country there are different work permits. Some are for those who work for companies and government organisations. Other work permits are for those who work as domestic workers. The domestic workers are not allowed to work for the companies without the permission from their Bosses."

I went to the man who kindly gave me a copy of his passport. I told him what happened. He said, "I don't know the boss who issued this work permit." He added, "My brother paid him to issue this work permit, and my brother is not here now, he is a truck driver who goes to very far countries."

I thanked him and went home. Since the company needed new staff to start work soon, I thought they would not wait for me for that long. With all the desperation for the job and the excellent chance I found and missed, I had to hold my breath back and continue the relentless struggle to find a job.

At that time, I was a bit more experienced than before. There was no chance for me to use my ID for work because of legal reasons. This time, I had to look for a man of my age who had a company work permit and ask to let me use his ID for work. Then try and find if there were any other chances of work.

With the living difficulties at home, we were all desperate to find jobs and there weren't many companies looking for workers and employees. We had to overcome two obstacles before succeeding in our endeavour. To find some IDs that we could use for employment and then find jobs. Both tasks were really hard to make them happen. Even though we knew that success was not within our reach, we had no choice but to keep trying. We divided ourselves into groups. One group went to an area of the city looking for jobs and the other to another area. We all came back in late afternoon and shared information about jobs. In the evening, the Somali men used to go to some Cafes to meet others. Many of the men were employed and others were unemployed. At the café, men exchanged information about how to survive in the country and any other important issues. Finding jobs for the unemployed was the hot topic on the table.

One evening I was at a café. I had a conversation with a man.

I told him about the chances I found and my disappointments.

He said, "Was it you whom I heard of?" Then he added, "Do you speak different languages?" I said, "Yes."

The man was of my age. He was sympathetic to me and promised to give me a copy of his ID card to help me find a job. I thanked him so much. From that day on, one of my big problems was solved. The next task was of course finding a job.

One morning, two men came to me and said, "We have heard that there is a company starting the construction of a new road. They are looking for workers. You can speak Arabic let us go and ask for jobs."

It sounded good.

Three of us took a bus to where the company was. When we reached there, we didn't see much work going on. We saw a few container offices. We went in and saw some men working in an office. We asked them if there were any job vacancies. Fortunately, they were happy to see us looking for jobs.

One of the men said, "We are starting a project here. We need some workers to help us settle and start work."

I said, "We are ready to work with you."

The man spoke to another one in the office and told him to recruit us to start work. After registration, the man who was a foreman for the company brought us out of the office and showed us some manual work that needed to be done.

He brought some construction tools: two spades and one hole-digger. He gave me a spade and told me to spread a load of sand in front of an office. Then he gave my colleagues the hole-digger and a spade and told them to dig some post holes to build a shed for cars. The man left us and went away. My two colleagues started to dig a hole, but the ground was hard for the hole-digger to penetrate in the earth. They tried to hit the ground harder and harder. The one who was hitting the ground with the hole-digger felt pain on his shoulders. The other one was even weaker than his friend, so he couldn't help. In addition to the hard work, the weather was unbearably hot in the desert. We were all alone working outside the offices.

They came to me and said, "We can't do this job, let's go and look for another one." I couldn't believe what I was hearing from my Somali friends.

I said, "I don't think that is a good idea, I think we are lucky to find jobs. So we shouldn't make this mistake."

They insisted and made their own final decision to leave. Honestly speaking, I hated staying in a country illegally, but understandably it was inevitable for me to do whatever I could to survive. Few minutes after my friends left, there I saw a man driving a car in front of the office. He stopped the car and came to me.

He said, "Where is the foreman?"

I said, "He has just gone."

He said, "Tell him, the project manager came to see you."

The man spoke English and his accent was American.

After a while, the Arab foreman came back and asked me, "Where are the other two men?"

I was a bit embarrassed to tell him that they didn't like the job and left.

So, I said, "They have probably gone for a drink."

Then I told him about the American man.

He said, "Who spoke to the American man?"

I said, "I did."

He said, "Do you speak English?"

I responded, "Yes and I speak other languages too."

He was pleased to hear that. He had a look at the job that I finished while he was away and said, "Well done."

After one hour or so, the foreman said to me, "Are your friends not coming back?"

I said, "They might have found another job."

He said, "I am going to get some workers."

After a while, he brought three workers in his car. He gave them a hole-digger and a spade. Then, he gave me a tape measure. He instructed me to check the depth and the width of the holes they were going to dig.

He said, "The holes should be forty centimetres wide and forty centimetres deep."

Since the project was a road being built, soon I became a member of the survey team. We had our own office, measuring equipment, and a car to carry our tools and equipment. The first hour of my first day was my last time working as a manual worker. Thanks to Allah the almighty. My hard work of educating myself had paid off. The construction work was going well and I got on well with everybody. Whenever I noticed that there was a need for a worker, I used to bring some Somali unemployed workers. The first was my cousin and then many more started to work for the company. Since many Somalis were unemployed my name spread amongst the Somali community.

I remember one particularly interesting story. A Somali man who was at least in his fifties came to the company I was working for.

He saw me and said, "Are you so and so" calling my name.

I said, "Yes."

He said, "I am a brick layer can you help me find a job here please?"

I took him to the office and I said, "This is my uncle, he is a bricklayer. Is there any vacancy?"

They said, "Ask him, does he know the bricklaying well?"

I asked him the question and he responded, "Yes."

The Somali man started working. After around four days. I was called by the foreman, whilst I was working at the site.

He said to me, "Your uncle is struggling to do his work."

I said, "What happened?"

He said, "He couldn't finish one job for four days."

I said, "I'll speak to him and see you later." I saw the bricklayer and asked why he couldn't finish one job for four days. After a short discussion, I observed his work and I found out that the man wasn't an experienced bricklayer. He wasn't even good at using his tape measure. I felt embarrassed because they were respecting me when they employed him. I went to the foreman and apologised for what happened and told him that the Somali man wasn't fully qualified for the job.

The foreman accepted my apology then said, "He can work as a helper." Then the Somali man decided to leave the job.

To me, that was a big damage to my reputation in the company. They always relied on my word and regarded me as a dedicated employee.

The road construction ended in one year and a few months. Our surveying group was allowed to stay with the company without doing anything. The reason was, they were waiting to finalise a contract with a company.

After a few months, we started working on a new site. This time, our company was a sub-contractor and the main contractor was a French company. We started building a site for the main contractor. It was going to be their main construction operations site. It was their offices and a massive garage for the construction hardware. A diversion road was in the plan too.

One morning while we were working on the site, a French man came to us. Since I knew the main contractor was french I greeted him in French. "Bonjour monsieur."

He smiled and said, "Bonjour."

He said, "Are you the manager?"

I said, "No, the manager is in the office."

He said, "I would like to speak to the manager, but I don't speak English and not Arabic either, could you translate for me please?"

I said, "I will."

The manager came out of the office while we were talking. I told the manager that the French man wanted to speak to him.

The manager said, "Does he speak English?"

I said, "No."

He said, "Do you speak French?"

I said, "Yes."

The manager was pleased to hear that. I turned to the French man and asked what he wanted to talk about. He asked some questions about how the work was going. The manager responded to his questions. In the end, both of them were grateful for my help. After that morning, there were some inspectors from the French company but they all spoke English. Our surveying work was going smoothly. We normally came in the morning and sat in the office until everybody came in.

Most of the time the foreman who was a new one came to our office, and whenever he entered the office, the whole team stood up for him, but not me. It was quite awkward for me and wondered why they were doing that. In our Somali culture, we stand up for our parents and elders. Other than those, we stand up for high-ranked officials but not company employees. I could see from his unusual stare at me, that he wondered why I didn't stand up for him. Since there was no chance for discussion about it, I just kept quiet.

One afternoon, whilst we were at work, it was my prayer time to go to a nearby mosque. At that time, the foreman was there with us, I asked him to let me go to the mosque, to pray. He didn't seem happy about it.

He said, "You can pray here" and pointed to the ground near us, that was filthy.

I said, "How can I pray here?"

Then he showed his unhappiness and said, "I don't know, I saw them praying here."

I was extremely astonished and realised that the man was an Arab, but wasn't a Muslim. To me, it was unbelievable; because that was my first time I saw an Arab man who wasn't a Muslim. I asked him, "Are you not a Muslim?"

He said, "I'm not a Muslim."

I said, "I am sorry, it's my fault because I asked you about my prayer, which has nothing to do with you." Then I went to the mosque. I came back to the site. I was surprised to see that there was no one at the site. Then I went to our office.

Our team and the foreman were sitting in the office. As soon as I came in, the clerk handed me a letter. I read it and understood that the foreman accused me that I had left the site without permission. There was also good news in the letter. It said I was allowed to go for my prayers for fifteen minutes whenever I needed to pray.

I asked the clerk, "Who wrote the letter?"

He said, "The manager wrote it." Incidentally, the manager was a Muslim, unlike the foreman who showed so much disrespect to my prayer.

Around three months passed since we started work at the new site.

Since our company was a sub-contractor, sometimes our jobs were less than what we used to do. As a result of that, some workers were laid off for redundancy. One morning before we started work, the clerk handed me a letter. It said that I was laid off. I immediately understood that it was the idea of the foreman, whom I knew, couldn't wait to get rid of me.

I went to the company's head office and handed in my redundancy letter to the human resources manager. Then, he sent me to the accounting office. The accountant gave me my outstanding payment. Then I went home. This time most of our group were working but one of us was going to Somalia.

After around a month of my redundancy, my friend who was getting ready to go to Somalia, asked me to go with him to the city to help him do some shopping. We went on a bus.

Before we reached the city centre we saw a police checkpoint. A policeman came on the bus.

He said, "IDs please." My friend got a card from his pocket but unfortunately, I had nothing in my pocket. The police caught me and my friend went on to the city centre alone.

Many people who were caught by the police and I were taken to the police station. Everybody was asked whether they had residence or not. From when the policeman asked me for an ID, it was quite clear to me that I was at the end of my stay in Kuwait. So, my mind was set to go to Somalia. When they asked me the question, I told them that I didn't have a residence. I also added that I wanted to go to Somalia. They kept us in the police station for a few days. Then they took us to a deportation centre. When I came in, I realised that most of the inmates were Sudanese men. They welcomed me warmly. They told me that the Somali men never stayed in the centre for long, because if they didn't have money to buy a ticket, their Somali compatriots would buy a ticket for them and went to Somalia. This culture is probably very rare in the other nationalities because this is a part of government responsibility. The Kuwaiti government never helped those who couldn't afford to buy tickets to go to their countries.

To my astonishment, the inmates were suffering from malnourishment, because they were not given adequate food. It was quite incomprehensible that the inmates were not helped to go to their countries and also kept in the deportation centre being not fed well. One of the horrible experience, I sow was, some of the men were skin and bones who could hardly stand up.

On the second day of my stay in the deportation centre, I had some visitors from my community who brought me some food and drinks. Everybody in our community knew how bad the inmates were treated. I stayed in the centre for about two weeks and a half to wait for my flight to Somalia. My cousin and my friends bought me a ticket and made some shopping for me. In the end, the day for me to fly home came about. I was taken to the airport by a policeman. The policeman was holding my passport and the ticket because I was being deported from the country.

After waiting for about two hours, it was time for the passengers to board the airplane. The policeman gave me my passport, then, I boarded the airplane. Our next stop was Abu Dhabi. After waiting for few hours for the flight to Somalia, It was time to board the Somali Airlines plane. Compared to when I was leaving Somalia, this time was completely different. I was feeling homesick. I realised how we Somalis were blessed with the best weather in the world and the fertile land. After living in the unbearable hot and cold weather for nearly three years, I realised the goodness of my country.

Chapter Six
The Brutal Somali Civil War
(Black Hawk Down)

Arriving from Kuwait, our Somali Airline plane landed at Mogadishu Airport. At the airport, there was no one to welcome me. The reason was at that time, in Somalia, telecommunication was quite limited.

However, I didn't feel that I needed someone to welcome me. It was fairly easy for me to take a taxi home. Home, sweet home! In contrast, it reminded me of the night, we landed at Kuwait Airport and the hardship we faced. My family was ecstatic to see me, and welcomed me warmly. I was incredibly relieved and felt peace in my mind. I was rejoiced by the pleasant weather of my country and the absolute delight of being with my people.

After a few days of rest, I went to the city centre to see how things were going. It was in June 1986. Everybody was trying to get on with their own business. The government was in control but some rebel groups were building up in neighbouring Ethiopia. My family was still struggling with their daily life. I came back with some money but not much. I had to make some changes to the level of my family's living. It wasn't easy at all, because when you have been away from your country for so long, it is impossible to find things easy.

At that time, I wasn't thinking of working for companies, but how to generate some sort of income for the family. Then buy a plot of land to build a house for the family to live in. I started to work in the currency exchange market in the city centre. Many foreigners were working with some organisations. The foreigners needed to change their currencies to Somali shillings. Also some Somali people wanted some foreign currency to use while travelling abroad.

After a while, I realised that so many people were in the currency exchange business, making prices highly competitive. I was making a bit of profit but not enough to cover my family's costs. I bought a plot of land and then decided to start work at the food market. At that time, my father passed away. May Allah forgive his sins and grant him his paradise? It was 1987. Whilst working in the currency market, I made some friends in the food market. When I was working in the city, I used to go to work early in the morning and come home in the afternoon but this time, I went to the food market early in the morning and came home in the evenings. Around one year or so had passed since I came from Kuwait. One of my brothers went to Saudi Arabia before I came from Kuwait. He was struggling with life, just like I did in Kuwait.

While working in the market, I had three things in my mind: Firstly, to keep supporting my family, Secondly, to build a house on the plot of land that I bought, and finally to get married, because I wasn't getting any younger but rather older. To achieve all three, was a real challenge. For about two years and a half of my return from abroad, my brother, in Saudi Arabia sent us some money. That was an excellent chance to build a house for the family. Since my next plan was to get married, I designed the house in a way that it could accommodate the family and also with my future wife and I. I built the house according to my plan.

I got on with my business in the food market. The inflation that started in 1981, when I left the country was ever-increasing, but this time, it was at its worst. When I bought some food stock intending to sell it at a bit higher price, the value of the shilling was changing dramatically. As a result, there was no profit to be made. That situation was making things extremely hard to survive in the market. In addition, I was thinking of getting married for an obvious reason. I decided not to waste any more time. I knew many would say, "What kind of decision is that, things are getting worse and worse and you are getting married?" That was a reasonable argument. But, I believe that we (humans and everything else) are in the hands of Allah. He controls everything. So everything will happen in the way he wishes.

I had to look for a wife who wanted to live with me and my family in the same house. The reason was that I couldn't afford to rent a separate house. After a long search, I was really lucky to find my wife with some help from a friend of mine who knew her well. I explained everything to her and she agreed. We got married at the beginning of 1990. There was a war that was going on in the northwest of Somalia which started in 1988. It was between the government and some rebels against it. There were also other rebels in the south of Somalia but not in and around the capital city

Mogadishu. I kept being optimistic. My brother, who was in Saudi Arabia, travelled to Norway, and sent a letter to me from there, then, I sent him a letter explaining the worsening situation of Somalia and the family in particular. After a while, he sent some money to us.

Since the government was getting weaker and weaker many people were fearful of civil war. They started to travel out of the country. Thinking in the same way, I decided to send two of my brothers out of the country. I told my brothers to go to Egypt and then contact their brother in Norway. They agreed and they went to Cairo. The political situation in Somalia was deteriorating, which made many intellectuals and elders worried and anxious. They decided to meet the government officials. However, unfortunately, we heard that the government wasn't listening to anyone.

We, the people in the city were hearing that the army was attacking people in some villages and towns, targeting some clans. The soldiers were killing people and burning the villagers' houses. The reason was, the government accused the people of being anti-government. The killing caused hatred and retaliation against the government by the people. Many military officials left their jobs and joined the rebels. The government was getting weaker. We heard that weapons were smuggled into the city.

Soon, we were hearing that some people were killed in Mogadishu during the night. At the banks, when people wanted to withdraw their money from their bank accounts, they were refused to do so. They were told to take a limited amount of their money. We were hearing that many government officials and their relatives were taking large amounts of money from the banks.

In the food market, where I was working, people didn't want to sell their food stocks with bank cheques. They wanted cash only. Some people who had cheques were forced to reduce the value of their cheques by thirty percent. That meant, if you had a cheque of one hundred thousand shillings you would only get seventy thousand shillings cash. The reason was the bank didn't have enough money to cash the cheques. Likewise, many people had foreign currency accounts in the bank. Those people with foreign currency accounts were given cheques, not cash. The values of their cheques were reduced too.

All government officials and their families were desperate to get out of the country. We heard that many high-ranked officials fought over airline flight bookings. Killing in the city increased day by day. We heard the military camps were attacked by the rebels. Military soldiers were leaving their bases in large numbers to join their respective clan rebels.

There were some talks between the government and some clan elders to save the country from a disaster of the foreseeable civil war. To our dismay the talks were unfruitful. That meant the war between the government and the rebels was going to intensify. People were fleeing to the towns and the villages to get away from the expected war in the city. Some rumours said, "Some weapons were smuggled from the military camps to the city," Which caused the ever-increasing insecurity in Mogadishu. All these abject actions culminated in the brutal war in the city.

One day, in the evening, there was a fight between some soldiers and some people in a part of Mogadishu. Some soldiers were killed, then, some military armed vehicles came to the scene. The military was shocked to see their armed vehicles destroyed with powerful weapons.

The war intensified hour by hour and day by day. Shells started to land in many parts of Mogadishu indiscriminately. People started to flee their homes not knowing where they were going. Family members ran for their lives not knowing who was they were with. Many were left helpless in their homes because they were not able to run or even walk. In the streets, people were stopped by the rebels or the government soldiers; they were being asked some utterly awkward questions. Many helpless civilians were punished or even killed depending on the fighter's judgment. No fighter was responsible to any commander.

My family and I were amongst those fleeing the war.

We decided to go to an area that was behind the rebels because the rebels were chasing the government soldiers. It was a long walk but safer than being in the war zone.

We started the journey early in the morning and reached our destination in the evening. Since we had nothing to eat, I had to go back in the next morning to bring some food from our house. To do so, I had to go through all the dangerous streets where the fighters of both sides were stopping and interrogating people. Then I had to come back on the same route carrying some food. Since we were a big family and didn't have money to buy food, I had to keep going back and forth to bring some food from home to the outskirts of the city. The war was going on for two weeks or so, and I was still going back and forth.

One morning, while I was going through an area held by the rebels, I had seen a terrifying experience. A pick-up vehicle passed in front of me. It was full of fighters with

AK47 machine guns. They suddenly pulled it up. They pulled down a man from the cabin of the vehicle to the ground and pointed a gun to his head. I didn't know any of the fighters, without thinking, I felt that I had to step in and stop the killing. I said "Stop" The man didn't stop the killing and the other fighters looked at me with anger and nearly shot me dead. I was really lucky, for I had no weapon. If I had one, they would have shot me dead.

They asked me, "Do you know the man?"

I said, "No but I am against any killing."

They said, "This man was a mass killer, so he had to be killed."

I couldn't bear what I saw and had to run away from the horrible scene. I went home, got some food, and then went back to my family. Many parts of the city were held by the rebels and the government troops were in few military camps and the presidential palace.

Many government offices were looted and destroyed. It was a real chaos. One morning, while going to bring some food from our house, I saw two men who were stopped by the rebels. They asked the two men some questions. I recognised one of them, then, I decided to tell the rebels that the men were not their enemies. Luckily they decided to let them go.

I kept walking towards our house. Our house was in the area held by the government troops. One of the rebel fighters saw me going to the government held area.

He called me and said, "Where are you going?"

I said, "I'm going to my house."

He thought I was helping the government troops and pointed his Ak47 at me.

I ran to him and said, "Stop pointing the gun at me." Then I explained and convinced him that I wasn't helping the government army. It was a scary moment that I felt helpless. The fighters with machine guns could kill whoever they wanted, having no fear of being held accountable for what they did. I came back to my family carrying some food. The war intensified for it was going in the city nearly for a month. We were extremely lucky to have been out of the war zone.

We were told that many people were killed in many parts of the city, held by both sides. We had also been hearing that the looting was getting worse and worse. There were no news reports because the information was controlled by the government. There were no private news agencies allowed. The only available news was the BBC Radio Somali language from London.

After around a month we were told in an evening, that the presidential palace was attacked by the rebels in their large numbers. Then the president and his troops had to flee the palace and Mogadishu altogether. Since we were staying outside the city, that night, we saw the whole sky filled with sparkling fired bullets. The rebels and their supporters were celebrating their victory over the government. In the next day, the city was ecstatic with joy. Nobody knew what was coming next. It was in January 1991.

The rebels were not organised to fill in the power vacuum. There were many different groups with their respective commanders and supporters. Many rebel fighters chased the government's troops to the Kenyan border. Large numbers of civilians went to the neighbouring countries: Ethiopia and Kenya. Many government buildings were looted. Many food storages were broken into. There weren't any authorities to stop the looting and all the ugly actions that were going on in the city. Some of the rebel leaders started to call themselves presidents. Despite some attempts of solving their differences, there was no success of reaching a deal. Since the military hardware was looted, everyone was heavily armed and controlled by no one. It didn't take long when killing civilians started in the city again.

Back to my family's story, we came back to our house. Our daily life was really bad. Many people were looting, then, selling what they found.

The prices in the market were very high. We stayed in our house, as we decided not to take part in what was going on. Sometimes, I tried to go to the market to find my friends who were still working in the food market that I used to work in. Fortunately, I found some of them. I was shocked when I found out that the traders had guns in their shops. After thinking about it, it seemed to be understandable, because there was no police to stop the criminals, so, the shopkeepers had to defend themselves from the looters.

After a few months, the power struggle intensified in the city, there was a brutal civil war among the factions who were trying to fill in the government power vacuum. Heavy fighting became inevitable. Large numbers of nomadic people started to move into the city. Since there was nothing for them to do, they started to operate as robbers and looters. Some of the brutal robberies they were doing were, stop the cars, kill the drivers and take the cars with them.

The civil war of Somalia was heard all over the world. The United Nation was well aware of what was happening in Somalia. The international community decided to help

Somalia end the disastrous civil war. Some multinational armies led by the USA were sent to Somalia.

One early morning, we heard that American soldiers came to Mogadishu by sea. The airport and the seaport were closed since the fall of the government. That morning, we saw some ships in the Indian Ocean. The airport was reopened by the Americans. Airplanes started to land. Ships started to dock on the Mogadishu seaport. We heard that the faction leaders were contacted by the United Nations envoy to Somalia. We also heard that the faction leaders reached some sort of agreement to stop the fighting. The civilians were desperate to see somebody who cared about the humanitarian crises. Some people started to starve to death. News reporters took some dis-heartening images of the Somali people.

Some international charities started to come to Somalia. They tried to distribute food to the civilians. Sadly, whenever the charities started to distribute food, some armed looters interrupted and started to take so much needed food from the civilians.

My family needed food but we couldn't even try to approach the charities, because of the danger involved. Instead, we decided to leave it and stay away. I always tried to go and borrow some food from some friends in the Bakara Market, in which I used to work as a trader. The situation stayed the same for many months. Luckily, no one in our family was hurt. Most of the families lost loved ones or were injured. Some families were all killed in their houses by shells.

One of the faction leaders wanted to control many parts of the city including where the United Nations were based and controlled. There was a fight between the faction leader's fighters and the UN army. Many UN soldiers were killed in the fight and the UN ordered the arrest of the faction leader. The faction leader hid in an unknown place; however, the UN was determined to arrest him. The faction leader ordered his fighters to stop any UN troops coming out of their camps.

When the Somali fighters tried to stop the UN troops, who were mostly Americans, the Americans used their heavy military machines. The heavily armed American military personnel could not stop the faction leader's fighters. Then the Americans needed to call their specially trained soldiers, who were called RANGERS to arrest the naughty Somali faction leader. The RANGERS decided to use helicopters called BLACK HAWKS. The real battle of Mogadishu started when the Somali fighters resisted the RANGERS. I thought the RANGERS were hoping their enemy would surrender when they saw the mighty weapons. The Somali faction fighters were supported by a large number of civilians. More American soldiers came to the Bakara Market, but they were stopped by the Somali fighters. More BLACK HAWKS came to help the RANGERS.

The faction leader fighters used Anti-aircraft machine guns mounted on top of tall buildings and shot down two of the BLACK HAWKS. Soon the other BLACK HAWKS went away. And the fighting had intensified. Then inevitably many American RANGERS were killed and the bodies were dragged in the streets of Bakara Market. Many American soldiers were trapped in the battle zone. They were fighting for hours and hours while surrounded by the Somali fighters.

After the Black Hawks were brought down and the RANGERS' dead bodies were dragged in the streets, some Somalis remembered their traditions of using their poetic verses on occasions like that. For those who don't know Somalia has a nickname "**The land of poets**." For occasions like that, the poets never miss to point out exactly what happens, whether it was sad moments like that or happy moments. On this occasion, they said,"**Rangersku ma rootiyaa rayadkiyaaba raamsadee?**" which roughly meant "**Are the RANGERS loaves of bread, the civilians are munching them?**" Before the RANGERS were brought to the battlefield, the media exaggerated their ability, so they were expected to out-perform their enemy. Besides, the Somali faction fighters were civilians and that was what the poet was trying to point out. A very much larger number of fighters and Somali civilians were killed too in the brutal battle. The fight went on and on for a day and a night.

Finally, a convoy of some other nation's troops of the UN came to the rescue of the Americans. They were heavily armed with TANKS. Fortunately, the trapped Americans were freed and taken to safety. There were still some American soldiers captured by the Somali fighters. Also, some dead bodies of the RANGERS were held by the faction leader fighters. The Americans started to negotiate for the release of the captured soldiers and the dead bodies. In the end, an agreement was reached for the American soldiers and the dead bodies to be released. Those days were the most horrible experiences of the Somali civil war. To see how this happened see this **YouTube video: Black Hawk Down: The Untold Story.**

QUOTE; Armytimes.com: 25 years later army leaders can learn from the harrowing battle of Mogadishu of 1993. By Todd South.

"Even to date, only a handful of battles over the past two decades even come close to matching the sustained intensity of that 15 hours fight in Mogadishu."

Back to my family's story, we were not far from where the fighting was taking place. A shell landed near our house, but luckily it fell on a sandy ground and didn't explode. The fearful sound of the bullets and the hovering Black Hawks were all over our house. I had told everyone in my family to sit in a corner of the rooms, so if a shell landed on our house, it could only kill some of us. Luckily, no shells landed on our house. We used to go out of the house, when the fighting cooled down. That was when we needed to do our shopping in the market. We had no money, but fortunately, I could still try to borrow some food from friends in the market.

We could have been getting some money from my brothers in Norway but there was no telephone service or banking system in Somalia. All international services were simply impossible to access. I remember when the airport was opened, I wrote a letter to my brother in Norway, to tell him how the situation was in Somalia. Since the postal system was non-existent, I went to the airport and saw a man in a car. He was going into the airport. I asked him whether he was going abroad.

He said, "Yes."

I asked him, "Where?"

He said, "Nairobi, Kenya."

I said, "Could you do me a favour please, and post this letter from there?"

He said, "I will do that for you."

I thanked him and asked who he was. Then he told me that he was a reporter for the BBC. Many years after that, my brother told me that the letter was an amazing news, not only for him, but for the Somali people in Norway at the time. He said, "I read that letter to a large number of Somali people in a bar." He added, "They couldn't believe how a letter came from Somalia, given what was happening in the country."

To find out more, you can see this. **BBC News 1st February, 2017 (video): Black Hawk Down: The Somali Battle that changed US policy in Africa.**

After that disastrous war, the US decided to pull out of Somalia. Then all the other UN-led troops and charities followed going out of the country too. The withdrawal took time. The battle of Mogadishu was on 3–4 of October 1993. The withdrawal was completed on March 3th 1994. Then, the UN troops' withdrawal ended on 28th March 1995.

After the **Operation Restore Hope** had been withdrawn, The Somali faction leaders kept fighting each other, being thirsty for power. Many attempts to reach an agreement failed. The Somali civilians, who badly needed a solution for the conflict, were the victims, who suffered the biggest loss. My family and I were obviously among them. One day a brutal fighting started in the area where we were residing. Our house and the neighbouring houses were under fire. Bullets were hitting our walls. Some fighters were hiding behind our house. We were caught between the crossfires. Luckily, the bullets didn't go through our walls. While panicking, we hid in different parts of the house to dodge the bullets or shells.

After a while, the fighting cooled down. We decided to escape the dangerous area. We couldn't take anything but our children. We were hearing the sound of the bullets but that was a bit far from us. We had to cross the roads, where some snipers were shooting at anyone crossing the roads. We lined up in a single file and made gaps between us whilst crossing the road. We did that, to avoid death or injury to many of us at once. Thanks, Allah, none of us was hurt, then, we reached a better place. That place was not far from Bakara Market, where the brutal Black Hawk down fight took place.

We felt lucky, but our children were crying because of hunger. For that reason, I had no choice but to go back and cross the fire-ridden streets to get some food from a shop in Bakara Market, where I kept some food for the family. To my delight, I came back unhurt. We stayed there for a day and a night sheltering under a concrete building with other people. Some people told me that our house was broken into and all our valuables were taken away.

Seeing that the area was not far from the war zone, we couldn't stay there for long. We heard that there was a better area. We decided to leave the crowded house. We left there early in the morning heading towards the other area. While on our way, we were stopped by robbers. They pointed a gun at us, then, told us to line up against a wall. They searched us and took our food that was in a sack. We noticed that they were planning to kill us. We all feared the worst, thinking they would kill us all.

Fortunately, one of them was against the idea and he let us go. We kept walking until we reached the safe area. We found a tall building that was abandoned. I told the family to wait there. I went around the area which was mostly deserted. I met a man who looked to be a resident in the local area.

I asked him, "Who is the owner of the tall building?"

He said, "The owner went to Yemen, but I am the caretaker."

I asked him if we could stay in the building.

He said, "I would be more than happy if you could stay there and look after it." He was right because looters were breaking into the empty buildings and took doors and windows.

We settled in the ground floor and other families came after us. They settled in the upper floors of the building. The fighting was still going but not near that area.

One day, I had a chance to go to a faction leader's palace. I heard that he had an international telephone connection. I asked if I could make an international call for a few minutes. I reiterated that the call could save the lives of my family. They let me make the phone call, which was very kind of them. In the phone call, I spoke to my brother in Norway. I explained the unbearable situation that we were in and told him that there was a trader in Dubai whom he could contact and send some money for us. My brother contacted the trader and sent money for us through him.

Chapter Seven
Scramble to Djibouti Adventure

After around two months, the trader came to Somalia. He brought much-needed food and other stocks. He gave me the money my brother sent us through him. Because of the ongoing problems in Somalia, we needed to find a solution for us to survive. For this reason, I decided to go to Djibouti, to be able to contact my brothers and then help our family. Djibouti is our neighbour and a brotherly country.

However, to go to it was not an easy journey, because it is very far from Mogadishu. Since travelling by air did not exist at that time, I had to travel by road via Ethiopia. I had given most of the money to my family and took a few hundreds of dollars with me. It was midday, when I took a pick-up vehicle that was going to a city called Jowhar. It is around ninety kilometres away from Mogadishu. Many other people and I travelled through a rough road. There were many militia-controlled stops on our way to Jowhar. They demanded money to let us continue travelling.

Finally, we reached Jowhar. I went to a bus station where I was told, I could find a bus that was going to Beledweyne, the capital city of Hiiraan. Hiiraan has a border with Ethiopia. That is where I planned to go first. From

Hiiraan, I could cross the border to Ethiopia. From there I could find a way to go to my final destination, Djibouti.

Luckily, I found the bus and travelled to Beledweyne. This time there weren't any militia stops demanding money. We reached Beledweyne peacefully. I stayed in a hotel for two days. I found out that some Lorries travelled regularly to and from Ethiopia. I found the station, and there was a lorry, that was going to Ethiopia in that afternoon. Some travellers and I were sat on top of the goods carried by the lorry.

We went to the Ethiopian border with Somalia. The Ethiopians stopped us and then allowed us to continue travelling into Ethiopia. The roads were extremely rough and torturous. Travelling through the unpaved roads made us worried. Sometimes that fear led us to get off the lorry, while going through big holes in the roads.

Finally, we reached a town called Qalafo. I stayed in a very small hotel for a few days. Then, I found a lorry that was going to Godey. A city belonged to the Somali region of Ethiopia. The Somali region in Ethiopia is vast. There was no road between Qalafo and Godey, but luckily it was a dry season, so we didn't have much difficulty. Driving on the unpaved road made us move so slowly.

In the end, we reached Godey in the evening. I asked for a hotel and found it. The hotel workers were friendly and welcoming. After having a meal and a good night's sleep, I woke up in the next morning. The weather was pleasant. I enquired about how I could go to Djibouti. They told me that it wasn't easy at all. The reason was, Djibouti is very far from Godey and the roads were not good.

They said, "You can go to Djibouti when you reach Dire Dawa."

Dire Dawa is a city that is not very far from Djibouti.

They told me, "From Dire Dawa you can take a train to Djibouti."

Furthermore, in the roads from Godey to Dire Dawa, there were Anti-Ethiopian government fighters, who stopped traffic and caused trouble.

I wasn't sure about what to do next. So I decided to stay for a few more days and try to find more information.

After three days, I was told that a military aircraft was coming to take some travellers to Dire Dawa. That was excellent news to hear. I inquired about where the airport was. They told me, it was in a military camp that was not very far from the hotel I was staying at. I went to the military camp. There was a big gate guarded by soldiers. I told them what I was looking for. They told me the military aircraft was coming on that day in the afternoon. Then, they asked me if I wanted to book a seat for myself. I said, "I would appreciate it if you could book me a seat." They asked me my name and told me to come back in a few hours.

I went to my hotel, had my lunch, and waited for a while. Then, it was time for me to go to the airport. I took a taxi and headed to the military camp, where the airport was. At the gate, there were many people, who wanted to go to Dire Dawa. I had a brief conversation with someone, who told me that there had not been an airplane coming to Godey for the last three months. That meant, we were lucky to find one.

The soldiers called the names of those who booked themselves earlier. I was called, then, went into the airport. The military camp was a big one. Many people were waiting to go to Dire Dawa.

After a long wait, the military aircraft arrived. Since the flight was a domestic flight, there was no immigration office or anything like that. The passengers lined up near the aircraft. Our names were already in a register. They called us one by one, then, we boarded the aircraft. Sitting in the airplane, I was relieved, because I was thinking of how difficult it was to come to Godey. I was also thinking of how hard it would have been if I were to travel to Dire Dawa by road.

The aircraft took off with no problems. The flight took around an hour to reach Dire Dawa. We landed at a small airport. It was just a landing ground. There weren't any offices. We got off the aircraft, and there we saw some taxis waiting for passengers. I took a taxi and asked if he could take me to a hotel. He took me to a hotel. I paid him and off he went. I came into the hotel. There I saw a receptionist, he checked, then, found a room for me. After settling in my room, I went out for a meal and came back. The hotel was very quiet and calm, so, was the area around it. I slept well in the night, woke up in the morning. I enquired about how I could go to Djibouti.

They told me that there was a Djibouti Consulate in Dire Dawa. From there, I could get a visa to go to Djibouti. Then, I could travel to Djibouti by train. They added that people go to the consulate early in the morning. At that time, it was half past eight in the morning. That meant I had to wait till the next morning. It was a good opportunity for me to go around and see the town. It was similar to the Somali towns with few differences. The people were from different backgrounds. Some were Somalis, some were Oromo people, and some were Amhara people. There were also some Arab origins. All those people had different cultures and religions. What impressed me was, they all co-existed and lived together peacefully.

The town was busy doing many different businesses. I enquired about international communication in Ethiopia. They told me that it wasn't as good as it was in Djibouti.

I came back to the hotel, stayed in for the rest of the day, and slept well in my second night. I woke up early in the next morning. Then, I went to the Djibouti consulate. There were so many people waiting to get a visa to go to Djibouti. I filled in a form and handed it in with my passport. There was something that I was concerned about. My passport was not genuine. It was made in Mogadishu illegally. The reason was all government offices were overtaken by tribal militias and they had destroyed everything. So there was no legal authority to issue passports. Earlier in Mogadishu, when we ran away from our house, looters took all our belongings. My passport was in a suitcase that the looters took.

I waited for a long time like everybody else. Finally, my name was called but the consular refused me the visa because my passport was not genuine. To me, the news wasn't surprising because the consular was right. I took a deep breath, sat down, and thought for a while. First of all, I couldn't complain. Secondly, I was genuinely desperate and needed a solution. These two facts left me with no option but to speak to the consular. I went to the receptionist and said, "Could I speak to the consular please?" The receptionist who was a lady, said, "Unfortunately, I can't do that, because we only do what he tells us to do, not vice versa." *Oh no! Another hurdle to tackle,'* I thought. I sat down wondering. When you face problems like that, you need some people to give you their thoughts. Many heads might be better than one. Sadly, I was alone. The big question was how could I go in and speak to the consular? After a long thinking and brainstorming, I came up with an idea. *'Since the receptionist did what the consular told her to do,'* I thought, *'write a note for the consular, ask her to put it in the visa applications pile.'* Then, he would be able to see my note. I asked her if she could do that for me. And she agreed.

Djibouti's official language is French but since my English was much better than my French, I wrote the note in English and gave it to her. I sat down and waited. After a while, my name was called, and then, I went into the consular's office. The consular saw me and raised his eyebrows.

He was negatively surprised and said, "Is it you who wrote this letter?"

I said, "Yes." I thought he was astonished by my appearance. That was because of the hardship that I was going through, for the long time I had been in the troubled Mogadishu. In addition, my good clothes were looted in Mogadishu in our suitcases, and couldn't afford to buy new ones.

I sat down and started to explain my problems. I had to confess that my passport was illegally issued, but I had no choice. I added that I was desperate to save my family's lives. I emphasised that it was about saving lives, not about illegal documents. I also mentioned the brotherly relationship between Somalia and Djibouti. A brother in need is a brother indeed. Somalia had never spared any effort to support Djibouti's success in their struggle for independence. I stressed again, that it was Djibouti's turn to stand up and help the collapsed Somalia.

To the credit of the consular, he was listening to me carefully and was incredibly sympathetic. He asked me some questions about the civil war and why a solution couldn't be found. I told him that if I was able to do anything about it, I wouldn't even spare my life to do so. He was really touched by the unbearable situation that Somalia was in. Since he was busy working and couldn't continue the conversation, he decided to help me and issued a visit visa for me. I shook hands with him and thanked him unreservedly.

I would like to see that man again, to thank him and celebrate what he had done to take his part in helping Somalia. From that day up to now, Djibouti had never hesitated to be at the forefront of any assistance to Somalia. I would love to repeat the slightly reworded English proverb. A brother in need is a brother indeed. I am Very sorry for the repetition. This story touches me so much.

I came back to my hotel then stayed for the day and the night. I was told that the train to Djibouti normally departed early in the morning. After a nice sleep, I woke up early, got ready, and took a taxi to the train station. There was a large crowd of people at the train station. Some were not travelling but they were selling things to the travellers. After a brief observation, I boarded the train. Although it was my first time on a train, it looked very old. It was overcrowded. The passengers were mostly traders who brought fruits and vegetables from Ethiopia to sell in Djibouti.

Djibouti is mostly rocky, mountainous, hot and dry. They rely on imports for their food supplies. Djibouti's location in the world makes it unique and strategically important. It is on the red sea, where a large number of ships go through every year. Furthermore, Djibouti hosts many international military bases. To view this visit: **China's military base in Djibouti/YouTube.**

The train was slow, so we reached the Border of Djibouti with Ethiopia in the evening. The train stopped at the border and our visas were checked. They stamped my passport with an entry. We continued travelling to Djibouti city. We were in Djibouti city in just a few hours. Djibouti was not a big city compared to some in the world. It had one train station. The population of Djibouti mainly consists of Somalis and Afars. There are also some Arab origins. While at the station, I saw some people from Somalia. I told them that I was new to the country and needed somewhere to stay. After some conversation, they took me to a house where some people from Mogadishu lived.

Somalia has many different regions. Since the civil war affected Somalia as a whole, many Somalis from the different regions of the country came to Djibouti for various reasons. If you were a new arrival, you would be taken to a house where people from your region lived. In the house, I met some people I knew in Mogadishu. There were men, women, and children in the house. In the next morning, I spoke to some of the people, discussing how the situation was for the people there. I noticed the house was overcrowded. They emphasised that living in Djibouti was unaffordable.

Seeing that the house was overcrowded, and others were expected to come from Somalia, we decided to rent another house. We went to look for it, then, we found a house that was suitable for us. Some of the people moved to the new house with us. The second problem that needed immediate attention was the food prices that they described as unaffordable. The people were new to the country so they had to go to the restaurants to eat, paying high prices. This was certainly a major problem that had to be solved.

I went to the city to find out how the most important matters could be done in the city. First of all, there was international communication system. The other important facility for us was money transfer systems. There were some banks. There were also a few Somali money transfer systems that had just started to operate. I enquired about embassies and consulates. They told me that the main countries of the world had embassies or consulates in Djibouti. The other important issue was the expensive living in Djibouti. Living in Djibouti was one of the most expensive in the world. The reason was everything had to be imported.

After discovering everything that was important to us, we started to deal with them in the best way possible. The first was the expensive living. I initiated an idea that could solve the problem. The idea was to stop going to the restaurants and start cooking our food at home. Then everybody agreed. That plan brought our cost of living down significantly. I saw a Somali man who had an international telecommunication shop. I told him we were a group of Somali people, who came from Somalia to contact their relatives and friends abroad. I added that we could sometimes need phone calls but would not be able to pay for it immediately. I assured him that the payment would be made when our relatives send us money. He kindly agreed, and I became the grantor, whenever there was a need.

Somali people are good at helping each other. One more important service that I secured was the incoming calls for our group. When one of us called their relatives abroad, they needed to receive calls from abroad, too. The only available telephone line was the one in the shop. So, I had to speak to the shopkeeper about that, too. The phone shop owner agreed and kept his promise. Whenever an incoming call was received, he sent someone with a message and told us, who needed to come to the phone shop.

We started to receive money sent by our relatives. The Somali money transfer shop became busy. I remember one day I received five hundred dollars from the Somali money transfer shop that was called Barakat. A few days later they called me again saying they had five hundred dollars for me.

I asked them, "Who sent the money to me?"

They told me that my brother sent the money to me. I realised that the money was the same amount that I received a few days ago. That meant they made a mistake. I told them that it was a mistake. The mistake showed that they were new to the money transfer system and needed to be careful.

Nowadays, the Somali money transfer system is one of the best in the world. If you send money from anywhere in the globe to Somalia or to anywhere else in the world, your beneficiary can receive your money within a few minutes from an agent or into their mobile phone. They are using some highly sophisticated programmes enabling them to move money with ease.

After a while, some of our people received invitation visas from different countries like Italy where many Somali people lived. I used to help those who needed interpretation and filling forms. The other embassies we used to go to were the USA, France, and the British consulate in Djibouti.

I thought of opening an account in a French bank. Then, I enquired about it. They told me it was possible. I opened the account without any difficulty. The bank account was helpful because there were some countries, in which Somali people lived, but there weren't any Somali money transfer agents. In that case, normal bank services were inevitable to be used. Then our people used my account to receive money from their relatives abroad.

I remember one day, I met a Somali man who came from Somalia. He heard that I was helping the Somali people who needed a bank account to receive money from abroad. He asked me to give him my account number and told me that he contacted a relative in Canada. The man in Canada wanted to send money to him but he had to find a bank account. I gave him my bank account. After around twenty days, I checked my account and noticed that four thousand dollars were credited into my account. The money was from Canada. I saw the man who told me he was waiting for some money from Canada. I told him that I had some money in my account that came from Canada, and the name of the man who sent it.

He recognised the name and said, "That is the man I was waiting to send me the money." I had more conversations with him and found out that he was a trader who came from Mogadishu for a business trip. I gave him the money. Then he went back to Somalia. After a few months, while I was in the bank checking my account, I was told that the bank manager was looking for me.

I went to the manager's office. He told me that there was some mistaken money that went into my account. I asked him how it happened.

He said, "Did you see the four thousand dollars that came from Canada?"

I said, "Yes."

He said, "That was supposed to be four hundred dollars but the bank in Canada made a mistake and added a zero by mistake."

I said, "Most of the money that is in my account belongs to other people, not me." I added, "I gave that money to a friend of mine who is a trader in Somalia. He comes here for business. I can ask him when he comes back."

The manager asked me if I was living in Djibouti.

I said, "Yes."

He said, "Please let us know when you see him."

After a month or so, the man who took the money came back to Djibouti. I heard that he was staying in a hotel. I went to the hotel and saw him. He welcomed me and was happy to see me. After thanking him for the welcoming, I broke the news to him. He was surprised to hear the news. I asked him if he had heard from the man who sent the money from Canada.

He said, "Not since I received the money."

I said, "You need to call him and ask him how much money he sent you."

Then he called him and learned that he sent him only four hundred dollars. Then, he gave me the three thousand six hundred dollars that was extra. I thanked him and went to the bank. I met the manager in his office. I told him that I got the money from the businessman from Mogadishu. He was pleased to hear the news, then, thanked me a lot. He told me to pay the money into my account and then they would deduct the amount I owed the bank from my account.

After securing the important services we needed to survive in the country, we also needed to communicate with our families in Somalia. Since there was no telecommunication system in Somalia, some traders in Djibouti came up with a solution for it. They brought some radio stations that could be used to communicate other radios in Somalia using frequencies. We started to call the radio operators in Mogadishu, and asked them to find and bring our families to the radio stations. At first, it wasn't easy but later the people and the radio operators got used to the idea.

In Mogadishu, there were some businessmen and women who wanted their money to be transferred to Djibouti, so they could buy some stock to ship to Mogadishu. Some Somali companies started airline business in Somalia. Ships started to carry cargo to Mogadishu and flights came from Somalia and went back. Soon all those much-needed services were available. Sadly, political differences had never been resolved.

Fortunately, some people hadn't given up hope and tried their best to provide services to the desperate Somali people. Those services were really useful to everyone. We could communicate with our people. We could send money to and from Somalia. We could fly to and from Somalia. We were relieved, and felt much better than before. Many people got visas to Europe and America, then, went to their destinations. Some people came from Europe and America to visit their families, who came from Somalia to Djibouti.

By that time, people used to ask me how things could be done in Djibouti. Including: Where the embassies were, the money transfer service offices, and the telecommunication services centres. I also had a good relationship with the airline companies. Apart from helping people, I used to receive money from my brothers and sent it to my family which was of course my prime duty.

One thing that I can't forget is that the Djibouti government didn't mind how long a Somali person could stay in Djibouti. We were not different to the Djibouti Nationals. Besides, when any Somali person wanted to travel abroad or back home, they were given an exit visa, no matter how long that person stayed in Djibouti. In addition, any Somali person or a group could set up a business in Djibouti without any restrictions.

Chapter Eight
Travel Abroad Adventure

In the end of February 1995, my brother who lived in Norway visited me in Djibouti. We had a long conversation about how we could help our family. I had hoped that the situation in Somalia could get better, but that hope was fading away. We were not hearing any good political news from Somalia. My brother came up with an idea.

He said, "You should go abroad, and when you get residence you would be able to claim for the family, and save them from the danger they are in."

For me, going abroad wasn't a good idea. But the memories of the brutal civil war in Somalia, which was never-ending, and the danger my family was still in, left me with no option. Travelling abroad wasn't an easy option either. There were many difficulties and dangers involved in travelling abroad illegally. When travelling illegally, life was at risk of being killed in some dangerous places. Furthermore, the cost of travelling was an uphill task. Risking my life was the ultimate price to pay, but because of the situation we were in, it seemed to be inevitable. In the end, our final decision was to risk my life to save our family. My brother gave me some money and went back to Norway.

In Djibouti, we used to see some Somali agents, who used to help those who wanted to travel abroad. The agents used to bring some documents with them. When the agents saw some people who wanted to travel, but couldn't find a matching document for them, they would go back to Europe and came back with some more documents. I enquired about the agents. Then, I saw a man who came to Djibouti to help those who wanted to risk their lives and their money going abroad. I had some conversation with him. He sounded optimistic and encouraged me to go ahead with my plan. He checked the documents he had and thought for a moment.

Then, he said, "At the moment I don't have a matching document for you, but I am going back to Europe soon," he continued, "I will try and find a matching passport for you."

I thanked him, then, I told him how he could find me when he came back from Europe.

I got on with my daily routine helping my people.

Occasionally, I was contacting my family in Mogadishu by radio. I used to ask them how the civil war was going on, and if there was any hope for it to end. They were telling me that sometimes the war stopped for a few days and restarted causing devastation. Whenever I asked them about it they were saying, "That is a part of our daily life, we are hoping that Allah will save us." It was distressful news but what could I do? I could only feel the pain as I knew exactly what they were going through.

The agent came back from Europe after being away for nearly two months. He came to me and told me that he had a passport that matched me. We discussed how he wanted to help me. His plan sounded reasonable. The plan had a few different phases.

The first phase was to apply for a visit visa to go to Dubai using the European passport he brought. There was another agent in Dubai whose job was to find visit visas. Then we had to go to the nearest city of Somalia to Djibouti. The nearest city was Borama. We had to make a fake Somali passport that had the same name as the one he brought from Europe. To the credit of the people of Borama, their area was peaceful, unlike Mogadishu. While in Borama, we made a fake Somali passport. We received a fax from Dubai. It was the visit visa that we were waiting for. The visa contained the nationality and the passport number of the European passport. The plan was to use the Somali passport while in Borama airport and while in transit at Djibouti airport. One might wonder, why did we need two passports? That was because, at that time, there weren't many Somali people who held European passports. Since there was no rule and no law enforcement anywhere in Somalia, the people there (Borama airport) could do whatever they wanted, so if they saw the European passport, they could take it from us or demand money. So the plan was to dodge them and avoid noticing we had a European passport. So we wanted to use the Somali passport while at Borama airport. The next step was to change the passport number and the nationality of the faxed visa copy to pretend that the visa was for a Somali passport holder.

The man went into a shop and asked if they had a typewriter. There were not many computers in Borama at that time. They kindly gave him a typewriter. He typed the word SOMALI and the Somali passport number. He cut the two from the paper and stuck them on the visa copy on top of the European nationality and the passport number with glue. Then, he made a copy of the visa fax which had the Somali Nationality and the Somali passport number on it. Next, he took the word Somali and the passport number off the visa copy. Now, we ended up having two visa copies. One was for the Somali passport and another for the European passport, which was the genuine one. For your information, the man had a Somali passport with a European residence, which was quite common to see at that time.

He bought a return ticket for me to go to Dubai. For his travel plan, he had a return ticket to Europe. He planned to go into transit in Dubai airport, and the other agent who found the visa for me in Dubai was going to pick me up from Dubai airport on my arrival. Our departure from Borama and the transit in Djibouti airport went well as planned.

While we were flying to Dubai, we had a meal, then, the agent told me to destroy the visa copy with the Somali passport details on, which I did and put it in the bin. Then, I hid my Somali passport in my handbag. After doing all those, I was left with the European passport and the genuine copy of the visa to enter Dubai.

We landed at Dubai airport. The agent reassured me that the job would be completed by the other agent in Dubai, then he proceeded to the transit and I went to the arrivals. At the immigration, I showed my visa copy to an officer, then, he took me to an office and found my original visa to visit Dubai. I lined up for the entry. Then, they stamped the entry for me. When I proceded to the exit, I saw a Somali man. He asked me, if I was so and so, Calling me with the name on the European passport.

I said, "Yes."

He told me his name and took me to a hotel in Dubai. Whilst on our way to the hotel, he told me that I had to stay in the hotel for five days. He continued, "The hotel was responsible for the visit visa."

As I understood, they helped people to get visas to enter Dubai with the condition of staying in the hotel for at least five days. So, that was why I had to stay there.

We arrived at the hotel reception. They gave me a room and took my passport.

They said, "We will keep your passport in our safe, here, until you are ready to travel and if you need we can give you a copy of it." I realised that the hotel was managed by Somali people.

I agreed and took the key to my room. The agent gave me his phone number and went. In the morning, I went out to see what Dubai City was like. I went to a Somali restaurant and saw some Somali people I knew in Mogadishu. After having some conversation, I told them where I was staying and what I wanted to do.

The next morning, my Somali friends visited me at the hotel reception. They accidentally called me by my real name, which made me a bit uncomfortable, because the receptionist could hear us. I didn't want the receptionist to notice my name was different to the one on my passport. I went out with my friends. They told me that some Somali people had tried to go to Europe. Some were caught, jailed and severely punished by the police, whereas others succeeded in their plan, and travelled to Europe safely. I called the agent and asked him about the next phase of the plan.

He said, "We will buy a ticket for you to fly to Europe."

After five days in the hotel, I moved to a flat where my Somali friends lived. After that, I met the agent again. We went to the hotel and asked them for a copy of the passport, which they gave us. He told me to wait for him until he found the cheapest ticket possible. I stayed with my friends exploring Dubai.

Dubai was a very busy city. There were so many businessmen and women from all over the world. Tourists could be seen everywhere. The tall buildings were amazing. Ships and boats were being loaded, carrying goods to all over the world. Shops and supermarkets were full of shoppers. The gold market was full of real glitter. Some of them sold diamonds. There was something I hated, which was the unbearable sweltering heat of Dubai desert. It reminded me of the years I used to live in Kuwait. People had to rely on air conditioning constantly. People couldn't stay in their houses, offices or in their cars without an air condition. While I was exploring Dubai, I saw some Somali businessmen, buying large amounts of stock, and shipping it to Somalia. I also saw some Somali people who were working for companies, whereas, others were working for the government organisations.

The agent came to me. Then, told me that he had booked a flight for me. We went to the hotel to get my passport. I asked the receptionist to give me my passport.

He said, "The hotel manager wants to see you." I went to the manager's office.

I said, "I'm told you want to see me, is that right?"

He said, "Yes, do you want your passport?"

I said, "Yes, I want to travel."

He said, "We know the passport is not yours," he added, "We have had some serious problems with people like you, who wanted to travel illegally." He continued, "If you are caught by the police at the airport, our hotel will be closed because we invited you to come to Dubai." He ended with, "I'm sorry."

I couldn't argue with him. So, I came out of the office. The agent was waiting for me eagerly. I broke the news to him.

The agent said, "The manager is right, if the police finds out about it, at the airport, the hotel will be in deep trouble." Then he added, "Don't worry, I can find a way to get the passport off him." He continued, "I will try and find another visit visa for you from somewhere else, then we can get the passport off them."

For me, it was scary, because I wasn't sure of what was going to happen next. My secret was discovered. I was wondering "Will the hotel manager tell the police?" Also "Will the agent find a visit visa for me?"

The agent had a copy of the passport. He told me to wait for him. He also insisted that I shouldn't be worried. I went home feeling uncertain about what was going to happen next. When we Muslims face difficulties like that, we turn to Allah and ask for forgiveness and help. So, I did ask Allah to help me. After all, my intention wasn't to cause any harm but to escape harm and save a life. I waited for the agent for at least a week, then, he came to me. Fortunately, he had a visit visa for me. We went to the hotel. He showed the visa to the hotel manager and said "Make a copy of it and from now on you are not responsible for this man's stay in the country." The hotel manager was happy to see my new visa.

Then he made a copy of it and handed me my passport. I was relieved, and felt fortunate. I thanked Allah, and then, the agent. We went to a restaurant, had a meal, and then, discussed about the next step to take. I missed the flight that the agent had booked for me earlier.

He said, "To use this visa you have to go out of the country and come back to get an entry." He added, "We will buy a ticket to Doha Qatar." He continued, "You don't have to go into the country. You stay in the transit at Doha Airport and fly back and arrive in Sharjah Airport." Sharjah Airport is not far from Dubai airport. The agent explained why I had to go to Doha. After some research, he found out that any non-white person holding a European passport was thoroughly checked at Dubai airport Immigration, before boarding any flight to Europe. The flight to Doha was to dodge the immigration officers because obviously, Doha is not a European country. I thought that was a good idea. So, I agreed. Then we bought a ticket to Doha. The next morning, the agent, my friends and I went to the airport.

I queued for the passport check to board the flight to Doha, Qatar. When it was my turn, I handed my passport to the immigration officer. He had a look at the passport. Then, he had a look at me. He called a policeman and said in Arabic, "Take him to the checking."

I was really frightened and nearly showed my fear, but I tried my best to hide it. The agent and my friends were watching me being dragged to the danger zone. What could they do? They could do nothing, but watch and wait for what was going to happen. While walking behind the policeman, I made my most sincere begging to Allah. This is the time when all humans say: "Allah help me, please! Or Oh God help me!"

The policeman took me to his commander and his assistant. He handed my passport and ticket to the commander. The commander gave my passport to his assistant. The assistant had a look at the photograph on the passport, checking whether it was replaced or not. He said in Arabic, "There is nothing wrong." Fortunately, the passport had not been fiddled with. At that time, the people who used to travel illegally changed the photographs of the passports to their photos. The commander's assistant was looking for any signs that showed the change of photograph.

The commander asked in Arabic, "Where is he going?"

The assistant had a look at my ticket and answered in Arabic, "He is going to Doha."

The commander took the passport and stamped EXIT. He handed me my passport and said, "Have a nice trip." In short, my feeling was indescribable. I went to the waiting area and rang my friends and the agent. They were pleased to hear the news.

I went to Doha and came back to Sharjah Airport in the afternoon. I called the agent from a call box in the transit area. Then he told me to stay in the transit area. He added, "I'm coming to the airport."

After an hour and a half, in the transit area, a uniformed Asian man, who was working in the airport called my name, then, asked me my passport and the airline ticket for the flight I missed before. The man told me, he was going to book a flight for me. I understood that he was sent by the agent. For your information, I left all my other documents in Dubai when I was going to Doha-Qatar. So, when I was at

Sharjah Airport, I had the European passport and the visit visa that the agent gave me. I didn't have any luggage but only a handbag with limited amount of clothes.

The Asian man came back and gave me my passport and two boarding passes. The flight he booked for me was scheduled in the next morning at ten o'clock, going to Stockholm via London Heathrow. I immediately called the agent from a call box. I thanked him, then, he told me what to do with the passport, when I reached my destination. He told me to destroy the passport before I saw the immigration officers at Heathrow Airport. I called my friends in Dubai and told them the news. One of them gave me the phone number of someone who lived in London. That night, I slept on a bench in the transit area. In the transit, there were so many people waiting for their flights.

In the morning, I got ready for my flight. Soon, it was ten o'clock. The airline staff called the passengers to board the airplane. We went in a queue and boarded the plane. We were told to put on our seat belts for take-off. That flight was going to a gulf state where a bigger plane was going to take us to Europe. We went to the transit area and waited for the next flight to London. Whilst in transit I went into a toilet and destroyed the visa paper which was the last document I had apart from the European passport.

After a little while, it was time to board the flight to Europe. We queued for a boarding check-in. We all went on a bus to take us to the airplane. While we were on the bus, someone came on the bus and came straight to me. He asked, "Can I see your passport?" I got it from my pocket and gave it to him. He had a look at the page where Dubai ENTRY and the EXIT were stamped. He gave it back to me.

We went on the plane. I took a deep breath. And said, "Thanks to Allah." what a relief! May Allah make the next step easy!

Once we were in the sky, flying to Europe, I didn't have much to worry about. I had heard about what was happening to those who managed to go to Europe and sought asylum. I was only thinking about following the instructions given by the agent.

The flight took a long time. My destination was Stockholm Sweden and my transit was London Heathrow Airport. When I was in Dubai, people told me that Britain was much better for asylum seekers than the rest of the European countries. The reason was that British people are more tolerant than the other European countries. In Britain, there are so many different people from all over the world, with different cultures and religions. So the British people got used to many cultures. The main reason for the tolerance is that Britain colonised many parts of the world.

For this reason, I made London my final destination. It was in the evening when we arrived at Heathrow Airport London. When we got off the airplane and walked into the airport, I was amazed by the size of the airport. I walked around for a long time. I was reading all the signboards. I didn't want to rush to the arrivals, because I was looking for a toilet to destroy the passport. I was following the instructions of the agent in Dubai. After walking up and down, I finally found a toilet and cut the passport into small pieces then flushed it down into the toilet.

After that, I went to the arrivals. There were so many people queueing for entry. Since I didn't have a passport and wasn't looking for entry, I didn't go into the queue. I sat on a chair near the queues. After around forty minutes, sitting on the chair, a man came to me, and asked me, "Do you have a passport?"

I said, "No."

He said, "Come with me."

I followed him. He told me to sit on a chair and wait for him. I sat there for hours. I was tired but wasn't worried. I was only thinking about what they were going to do next.

The same man came back to me and asked me, "Where do you come from?"

I said, "Somalia."

He said, "Do you know someone in London?"

I said, "Yes." Then, I gave him the name and the phone number of the person that my friend in Dubai gave me. He went away and came back after a long time. He asked me some questions. Then, I answered all of them. He went, then, came back to me and gave me a letter. The letter said that I was accepted as an asylum seeker. The man told me I could go and meet my friend at the arrivals. After around an hour, my friend came to pick me up from the airport.

Chapter Nine
UK Life Adventure

My friend lived in North London. I stayed with him. Then, when I had the opportunity, I called my friends in Dubai, Djibouti, and my brothers in Norway, to let them know that my travel adventure had ended in success and I had peacefully arrived in London. While staying with my friend, I asked him how I could live a decent life in London. He told me there were two opportunities that I could choose from. The first was working in factories and warehouses; the second was studying at a college. It was hard to make the right choice. However, the information was helpful. I thought about my family and how I could help them. I thought about my future life in the UK.

In the meantime, I visited many parts of London and I was amazed by the city and how busy it was. I wondered, how I could understand, how the countless businesses and activities were ran and managed. After I thought long enough, I decided to start studying at college, because studying and reading about everything was the key to understanding the systems used in the UK. There was also another reason that made studying a strong choice. It was my age.

I came to London in 1995; I was forty years old. If I chose to work in the factories and warehouses, how long could I continue working? Obviously, not very long, let's say, maximum of fifteen years, which was not a favourable working time limit. Alternatively, after studying for some years and being qualified, I could work longer than that.

My unsolved problem was my family's financial needs. I called my brothers in Norway and told them about my studies. Then, I asked them if they could keep sending money to our family in Somalia, while I was studying. My brothers agreed to the plan. I went to a college and enrolled. They assessed my English. Due to lack of practice, my written English was better than my spoken English. They told me that I could start a course because my English was enough to study. They also advised me to read English books to improve my English language skills. The course I chose was business studies. Business studies teach many useful aspects of management. It helps the learners understand modern life systems. I liked it and enjoyed studying.

While studying and concentrating on it, I realised that living in many parts of Europe and America was a challenge to everybody. For many people, making the right choice for their future life was difficult. Some people thought life was easy in Europe, however, their misunderstanding led them to fail in life and never been able to recover. Some people understood that only hard work and being careful about making decisions was important. Those people's understanding made a difference and led them to succeed in life. This is why I call living in the UK an adventure.

I saw some people who chose to work full time and bought cars. It was tempting, but I was determined to stick to my plan of studying.

My classmates at the college were mostly youngsters who were born in the UK. Since I was very much older and new to the country, I looked and sounded like a stranger in the wrong place. When I wanted to say something about the lesson, I couldn't express myself quickly, because my language fluency was yet to come. When the youngsters realised the difficulty, I had they laughed at me. Very little they did know that I didn't feel alienated, because I knew I was in the wrong class at the wrong age. Very little did they know that being in the wrong class was a big opportunity for me!

I remember, when I was doing my assignments, my tutor used to read them and found many language errors, nevertheless, she always liked my way of writing and my ideas. She used to say, I expect from you what I don't expect from others. Obviously, the reason was my experience in life.

In the college, I saw some people who were new to the country. They used to come and leave after a short time in a course. To me, that meant a lack of determination to study and reach a goal. I finished my first year with a pass, which was sufficient to proceed to my second year of the course.

In my second year, there were new arrivals who were mostly youngsters. When they were talking to each other, they used to say, "The lesson is boring." The youngsters were in a different world than the one I was in. For me, the opportunity to go to class and study was a dream comes true, but for the youngsters, it was boring.

Again, this is one of the reasons why I called this chapter an adventure. Just like those youngsters some adults think living in the UK is easy, with no difficulties. These people are making serious mistakes, which will eventually lead them to a disastrous life or at least very hard life.

In my second year of college, the assignments got harder. However, I made some progress. Even though I was on a job seeker's allowance and my income was very limited, I tried to learn how to drive. Before I started the practical driving, I started reading the driving theory book. It was much easier than the practical driving.

I applied for the driving theory test. I passed in the first attempt. I started to have some practical driving lessons. It was inconsistent due to my limited income. The inconsistency made me forget what I had learned and I had to restart learning the previous lessons all over again. Meanwhile, I was determined to follow my plan, which was to work hard to get a qualification and pass the driving test. In my second year in college, I completed my assignments and passed my exams.

I kept having more driving lessons. Then, later I booked a driving test. The examiner was a lady. I started driving, while she was sitting next to me. She had a book and a pen, noting any mistakes I made. I was trying to show her that I was a safe driver. When I came to a junction, I stopped and waited to make sure no traffic was in front of me. Then, I kept driving. In the end, I drove to the driving test centre.

The lady shook her head and said, "Sorry, you have failed." The lady handed me the result and told me that I was checking too much. She made it clear that the drivers behind me were delayed by my driving inability. She added, "You have to consider the drivers behind you as well as those in front of you."

To me, the comments were reasonable. I took the comments as a lesson. The questions on the test paper were fifty-two. The rules for passing were: No major mistake was allowed, whereas, if you made three minor mistakes, they were considered as a major mistake, which resulted in a fail.

It wasn't easy to pass, but resilience was the only solution. So, I had to be optimistic and keep trying.

In the college, I started my third year which was my final year. It was harder than the other two years. I had to carry out some business researches. I went to some business companies. Then, I interviewed managers, and recorded some questionnaires. Then, I wrote reports about their businesses. In the end, I piled up a portfolio of assignments. There were also a few examinations. In that course, I gained so much knowledge which helped me understand how most of the businesses in the cities were run. I could call it an eye-opening course.

Once I got that, I needed to go on to higher education to reach my goal. I spoke to my tutor about going on to higher education. She encouraged me to follow my ambition of going to university.

Meanwhile, I continued having some more driving lessons. I also booked some driving tests, but unfortunately, I failed to pass them. On some driving test occasions, I felt cheated by some examiners. I noticed they were trying to fail me without a clear reason. One of those occasions that I could never forget was, when an examiner was testing me. He couldn't find any faults except a minor one. But, because he was determined to fail me, he told me to go back to the same spot, where I made the minor mistake three times and finally told me that I failed, because of those three minor mistakes. That situation caused me some concerns about succeeding in my driving ambition. In my life time, whenever I encountered similar difficulties, I always tried not to give up but to persevere.

I applied to six universities in London, then, four of them offered me a place. I went to all of them to see which one was the best for me. In the end, I chose one of them. That was in central London. It had many compasses in London. I enrolled and started my favourite course business studies. After that, I received some money as a student grant. The money wasn't enough to cover my costs like rent etc. However, once I got the student grant my housing benefit was stopped. Also, my job seekers allowance was stopped. I had to stay with a friend of mine who was living in a two-bedroom flat. With all the hard work at the university and the tight financial difficulty, I had to keep trying to pass my driving test. What was worrying me was my driving theory test certificate, which was going to expire.

I decided to buy a cheap car, for I needed more driving practice. I bought an old car that costed me around three hundred pounds. I insured it, then, asked my friend to be my instructor. I used to drive it in the weekends, when the streets were less busy. I remember one day, I was driving without my instructor. A police officer noticed that my driving was not good enough and followed me. I saw the police car coming after me. After a while, I panicked and made a mistake. Then the policeman stopped me.

He said, "Do you have a driving licence?"

I said, "No."

He said, "Why are you driving?"

I said, "I'm going to my instructor."

He asked me for an ID. Then I showed him my university ID.

He said, "Leave the car here and bring your instructor to help you drive."

I said, "OK." then I thanked him.

I left the car there and after a while, I came back and drove it home. The policeman was kind to me because he could have taken legal action against me.

To go to my university, I used to take a train from North London to Central London. The nearest train station to where I lived is called Seven Sisters. In the morning, the trains were very busy. Oxford Circus train station was my final destination. When coming back in late afternoon, it was even busier. I used to go from one compass to another at the University of Westminster. Sometimes I had to go to the university in the evenings for seminars and some research work for my assignments. Some assignments were done in groups. As a group, we used to meet and discuss how we could do our assignments.

We had a lady lecturer who taught us a module called interpersonal skills. One day, she wanted to comment on me and asked me, "What do you want to do when you finish your course?"

I didn't answer her question. Then she said, "I don't think you are going to pass this year."

I was stunned for a moment and asked her, "Are you making your decision even before the examination?"

She did not give me an answer. She used to mark my assignments and made sure she gave me at least two marks short of the pass marks. For instance: if the pass mark was 40%, she gave me 38% without any wrong marks or comments on my assignments. The module had four assignments. Three of them were marked by her, but the remaining one was marked by another lecturer, who gave me high marks. To my delight, the average mark of the assignments was PASS. It was one of the hurdles that showed how life wasn't easy. No matter how hard you try, there will always be some people who will try to make you fail, but I was determined not to give up.

Back to my driving practice, after being busy with my studies on the weekdays, I used to practise driving my car early in the morning in the weekends. I would remember and try all the lessons that my instructor used to teach me. I practised the different ways of parking, the reverse corner, the emergency stop, the three-point turn, the observations, etc.

This made me feel confident and much better than ever before whilst driving on my own. I started to go to some places, driving my car to see some friends. Since my driving theory test was about to expire, I booked a practical driving test. This time I didn't have much hope to pass. The reason was those examiners who let me down so many times. In my past, I used to hire and pay a driving instructor and his car, but this time I decided to use my own car for the test. Also, I spoke to one of my friends to pretend to be my instructor and go with me to the driving test centre.

We went to the driving test centre, then, my friend sat next to me. The examiner came out of the office. He took me to the car park and asked me a few questions before we went into the car. I answered the questions, then, we got into the car. I drove off with confidence without being optimistic. I was driving, considering him as a passenger. He was giving me the instructions he wanted, and I was doing all of them without any hesitations. None of the questions seemed to be difficult. We came back to the driving test centre. I parked the car.

He looked at me and said, "Congratulations you have passed."

I couldn't believe what I was hearing.

He added, "Is this your first time?"

I said, "This is my ninth time."

He stared at me with an unusual look, and asked me to tell him my details off by heart. He asked me to spell my name, address, and everything else he needed to write down about the test result. I thought he was thinking that I was representing somebody else. To show him I was the right candidate, I spelt all the details without showing him that I understood what he was thinking of. I passed that test in February 1999. Looking back, I thought of how long it took me to pass? Since I was trying to make a quick progress, I was booking the driving tests every time it was possible. Later I realised that there were some times that I wasn't fully prepared to be tested, which lead me to fail many times. However, as I mentioned earlier, there were some occasions that I felt cheated.

Finally, I was glad to have passed and took one step of success in the UK life adventure.

Back to my business course, at the University of Westminster, after the summer holiday, I started the second year of my course. I felt that I was making some progress. The start of the second year was going smoothly.

This time, I was thinking of my family and how I could claim for them. I thought of the hard work. And the clear evidence of the progress I was making. I could prove that I was able to look after my family. I rang a lawyer and asked him if he could help me claim for my family. He asked me where my family was. I told him that they were in Addis Ababa, Ethiopia. He asked me to send him all their details, which I did. He sent the claim to the British High Commissioner in Addis Ababa. Then, I told the family to go to the British High Commissioner.

Whilst waiting for the claim, I kept working as hard as I could on my assignments. The course was to be completed in four years. After successful completion of the second year, there was a year of work placement for experience. The experience year was exempted from the mature students, who could demonstrate their business experience in an assignment. I asked my tutor to give me the exempt assignment, which he did. I successfully completed the exempt assignment, then, I was exempted from the work placement year. When I was around halfway through my second year of the course, The British High Commissioner in Addis Ababa refused the visa for my family to come and join me in the UK. The reason was that I wasn't working and I had no accommodation for them. It was disappointing and depressing, which made me sleepless for a few nights. I thought of how long I was studying and what I knew about the subject I had been studying for five years. I thought about the family and my children's future. Some of my children were already in their teens and were without education for a long time. I thought of my employment. I could be employed or be self-employed. The only thing that I didn't have was a business degree.

In the end, I decided to postpone the completion of my course and start work, to be able to claim for my family. I went to my course leader's office and told her that I had a family problem to solve. Adding, it was urgent.

She said, "You can come back and finish your course when you are ready."

I thanked her and went home.

The hard work I was doing was immediately diverted to looking for work. Since I had a car, I could travel for some distance to find work. I was told that there was a chance to find work in an industrial area outside London. I went there to try to find work. After visiting a few companies, I found a company with some vacancies. They interviewed me and observed that I could help them do their work much better. This was because I demonstrated my business knowledge. The company's work involved parcel delivery services. I was given the job of quality control officer at the parcel sorting centre at Hatfield Town Business Park. The centre was massive; there were around one hundred Lorries, coming in and going out every night.

After a good introduction and training, I started to control how the work was going and the workers were handling the parcels. If anything was not done well, I used to make sure it was rectified. I used to report to my manager, whenever there was a need to do so. My shift was at night. I used to start in the evening and finish in the morning.

I remember one early morning when I was driving from work to North London. The roads were nearly empty. Two policemen were driving behind me, but then, they noticed that my steering was a bit wobbly or I wasn't steering perfectly.

They stopped me and said, "Were you drinking during the night?"

I said, "No."

They said, "What were you doing?"

I said, "I was working for ten hours."

They had a machine for testing those who drink and drive. They asked me to blow air into the machine, which I did. They realised that I wasn't drunk and let me go. Even though I wasn't doing any physical work, the night shift was tiring. I agreed to work at night because it was the only shift that was available at the time.

After six months of work, I visited my family in Ethiopia. Then I returned to work.

The next step I had to take was to find accommodation that was enough for the family. In London, that was impossible because of the high cost of renting a house. I called some of my friends, who lived in some parts of England, to find out the rent of a three-bedroom house. The other important thing was finding a job from where the house rent was cheap. It was a challenging puzzle. I had to keep enquiring before I left my job. One of my friends who moved to Manchester told me that Bolton had the cheapest house rent compared to other towns. He also told me that there was a possibility of finding a job. I thought about it, and said to myself: "When you are looking for something you have to take some risk and rely on Allah's help for success." I decided to go to Manchester and see my friend, so, I took a coach to Manchester. My friend met me at the coach station. I stayed with him for the night, then, we went to Bolton in the next morning. Houses were available in Bolton, and the rent was cheap compared to anywhere else we had heard of.

I went back to London and made my final decision, which was to move to Bolton. I resigned from the Hatfield job. It was early in the morning on a weekend day, when I loaded my most important belongings into my car and headed to Manchester. Since I was not used to driving long distances, I was driving in the slow lane. So, it took me four hours to reach Manchester.

Manchester is nearly two hundred miles away from London. I came to my friend's house, stayed with him until I found a house to rent in Bolton. Then I found some single men, who wanted to share a house with other people. For me, that was helpful, because my family's reunion claim was going to take time. When my family got the visa and were about to come, I could let my housemates know. Then, they would find another house for themselves. I tried to find work. This time, I wasn't looking for a good job, but any job to prove that I was working and I had accommodation for my family.

It wasn't long before I got a parking attendant job in Bolton. They gave me a permanent job agreement. The two conditions that I wanted to fulfil were then in my hands.

1) Tenancy agreement. 2) Permanent job agreement. Then, I was ready to start the claim for my family. I sent the copies of the documents to my family in Ethiopia and told them to take the documents to the British High Commissioner in Addis Ababa. The British High Commissioner started to investigate whether my family and I were related. It was all about our DNA that needed to be

checked. That process took a very long time because they had to take my DNA sample and my family's DNA sample, then, find out whether the two matched. We were waiting for the result for months. After around ten months of waiting, I started ringing the British High Commissioner in Addis Ababa. There was an Ethiopian secretary who picked up the phone and never gave me the information I needed.

I thought long and hard as to how I could get help for the problem. Later I had an idea, which was, to go to my local member of parliament and ask for help. I went to their office in Bolton. There was our local MP's assistant in the office. I told him about my problem. Then, he asked me about the details of the claim. He made some copies of the documents and promised me he would send them to London where the MP (Member of Parliament) was working. After a month or so, my wife called me from Addis Ababa, saying, "The British High Commissioner called us and said, 'Come for your visa'."

After a few days, I received a letter from my local member of parliament. It said that my MP asked the British Foreign Secretary to explain why my claim took so long to make a decision.

I imagined that the Foreign Secretary sent a letter to the British High Commissioner in Addis Ababa and asked about my claim. I thought that the letter made them look at my claim and then had to call my family. My family went to the British High Commissioner then, they were asked to pay the fees for the visa. The family consisted of five persons. They had to pay four hundred dollars per person. That amount of money was too much for me and on top of that, I had to pay for their airline tickets and other small expenses needed when people were travelling from Ethiopia.

I sat down and thought about how I could cover all that cost. On one hand, I was happy because my family eventually got their visa; however, on the other hand, I was unable to send them the money they needed. After I had been thinking long and hard, I figured out an idea. The idea was to speak to some good friends, I made while I was living in Bolton. I told them about my problem and the money I badly needed and promised them I would pay them back as soon as possible. They were really sympathetic and very kind. Every one of them decided to lend me some money. I sent the money to my family. Then, they started their preparation to come to the UK. It took them around a month or so, to come and join me in Bolton UK. Just before my family came, my housemates moved out and found other homes for themselves.

It was a hard mission and many thanks to Allah. I also thanked my friends who gave me an invaluable helping hand. I started to pay them back one at a time until I completed. In life, when you accomplish one mission another one comes up until you die, and that is life.

Once my family joined me here in England, I had to try and help them to build their future. Two of my sons were already in their teens. They didn't have a chance to go to school before, because of the Somali civil war. In Bolton, they started to attend high school. They had to sit in a separate room and read some basic -English with a teaching assistant, while their peers were flying high studying. I was busy working and their mother cooking and cleaning and of course educating them as much as we could.

The family tried hard to get used to the life of the country. In a way, they were happy to join me, but they also had to learn a whole culture and a new system of life. The first obstacle was the language. I had to be with every member of the family when they wanted to sort something out. For example, neither of them could go to a shop to buy something. They weren't even able to pick up the phone and answer a call. The only work that I was not concerned of was the housework which my wife could do independently.

After a few months of my family's arrival, the company that I was working for, lost their contract, then, laid off their employees in Bolton. That meant, I had to apply for a job seeker's allowance, which I didn't apply for, for many years. To be eligible for a job seeker's allowance, I had to be actively looking for a job. It wasn't long before I received a letter saying, "We are pleased to inform you that you are entitled to receive a job seeker's allowance." Once a job seeker's allowance was allowed, my family and I were also entitled to a housing benefit and other benefits too. This is a remarkably useful system. It is a system that makes people help themselves, and each other, involuntarily. The government controls this system effectively.

In the meantime, some leading members of my community and I decided to establish a community centre. We started helping our community. Many people came and used the service we were providing and thought it was helpful. Those who were new to the town established a new life and got used to the system. Once the community centre was up and running, many members of the Somali community moved to Bolton and settled. We helped them find jobs and schools for their children. Those who settled in

Bolton called their friends who lived in Europe and told them to come and live in Bolton. Many families brought their children to the community centre to do their homework, and get the help they needed. The new arrivals from Europe contributed some useful skills to the community too. We, the founders of the community centre, showed our will to help the new arrivals to the town.

We also tried and eventually brought some skilled Islamic studies teachers, who helped the community to be good citizens. Everybody was committed to promoting the peaceful, progressive Islamic culture. Those combined services attracted more and more new people to Bolton.

The Somali communities in Europe found out that Britain was and still is more tolerant in accepting differences in culture, religion, and many aspects of life, than the rest of the European countries. That is why you can find lots and lots of people who initially settled in other European countries, decided to live in Britain. In our Somali community in Bolton, my family and I are in the minority of those who identify themselves as Somali-British and the large majority are from mainland Europe.

This reality reminds me, when I was studying in London we were asked to investigate why Britain is unique and attractive to so many people in the world. After a thorough research, we found out that the reason was, that Britain tolerated and accepted the various cultures of the world. Many believe that the tolerance was a result of Britain's colonisation of many parts of the world, then, they learned a lot about the world's cultures.

What many might not know is that the acceptance of the other nationalities to the UK doesn't only benefit the foreigners, but also benefits the host people and their government. These foreigners bring their skills and expertise to help the country's economic growth.

I had heard that many Somalis used to live in Holland, but they were not allowed to do most of the jobs. Then, some Somalis from Holland came to Britain and found out that there were no such restrictions like in Holland.

Following the good news, a large number of Somalis decided to move to Britain. Then, they started to do so many different jobs. The jobs included: driving buses, teacher assistants, social workers, taxi drivers, self-employed shopkeepers, and many more.

I was also told that Holland authorities heard about what the Somali-Dutch nationals were doing in Britain. Then some Dutch TV reporters came and interviewed the Somali people from Holland, who started a successful life in Leicester. The report confirmed that they were doing well in Britain, then, the Dutch were disappointed. In Bolton, we had our share of those arrivals from Europe. Those families and their children, who are now grown-ups, are still here taking part in the progress and the good livelihood of the country.

Back to my personal story, apart from the voluntary work for the community, I was actively looking for a paid job. My children were going to different schools. Two of my sons were in high school, whereas one was attending a primary school.

One day at around 11 AM, my mobile phone rang. I picked it up, then, someone said, "This is Brandwood Community Primary School, your son is in trouble, can you come to the school, Please?" It was the primary school where my son was attending. I rushed to the school to see what happened. I went into the head teacher's office and saw my son sitting there with the headteacher and her deputy headteacher. They told me that my son was misbehaving a lot in his class. I tried to explain to them that my son was new to the education system. Also, the other members of my family, who were all new to the country, were having difficulties getting used to the language, and the system in the country. Since I used to be a teacher in Somalia, I started to point out some ways of solving the problems like that. The head teacher seemed to be impressed with what I said. Then, she said, "Can I ask you a question?"

I said "Yes."

She said, "Are you working?"

I said, "I am not."

She said, "Are you willing to work with us?"

I said, "I would love to."

She said, "Bring your documents tomorrow and let's take it from there."

I thanked her and went home.

In the next day, I took my son to the school and then went into the headteacher's office. I handed my documents to her. She had a look at my documents. We had some conversation about what they wanted me to do.

Then, all of a sudden, there came a Somali family who was new to Bolton. They brought their son to the school, but he was having difficulties following the instructions of his teacher, and getting on with the children in his class. He told his parents that he wasn't happy with the school. The Somali parents of the child couldn't speak English.

The headteacher looked at me and said, "This is one of the problems, I want you to sort out."

I met the family before in our community centre on a few occasions. I told them that I had just started to work with the school and wanted to build good relation with the school and the community. The family was really happy to hear that. Then, I asked them what the problem was, and what they thought about the school. They explained the problem, their son was having, and what they thought about it. I told the headteacher what their concerns were and also that they recently came from Holland to live in Bolton. That was why they had difficulties communicating in English. Similarly, their son was not able to understand the teacher and speak with his peers.

I explained that obviously, the new arrivals needed some sort of welcoming plan until they got used to the school system. The headteacher was really sympathetic and promised that they will do something about the matter. Then, I explained to the family what the school was going to do for the new arrivals. Also, I assured them, I would keep an eye on their son. The family was thankful for the good service they received, and went home having much better thoughts about the school. The headteacher was pleased by how the problem was solved. She said, "You have done your first job."

After that, I was given the job of a teaching assistant, and to solve similar problems when they arose. I wasn't planning to work with a school in the UK, but it was coincidental. The school needed someone like me, and I was eagerly looking for a convenient job. It was a job that I was able to do with ease. The community, especially, the new arrivals needed my service to have confidence in the education system. I felt I was doing the right job, at the right place, at the right time, which I am still doing happily.

So, it is worth mentioning the date I started the work. It was on 17th May 2005. Since I was doing a voluntary work at the community centre, and also needed some time for my family's needs to do in town, I asked the headteacher if I could work part-time, which she agreed. I was given a timetable for my work. It is still more or less the same as I am writing these life stories. In the morning, we withdrew the pupils who were less able to cope with their class work. Then we taught them some basic-English, to enable them to catch up with their peers in class.

On some occasions, the office would call me to phone some non-English speaking parents and explain some things that needed to be clarified. In the first few years, the non-English speaking families were Somalis, but later we had some families who came from Italy. Since I was teaching basic English, the Italian-speaking children were brought to me. Then, I told them that I spoke Italian. The children and their parents were delighted to see someone who spoke Italian in their new school. The headteacher and the teachers were also happy to know that I could help them when they needed Italian interpretation.

A Few more years passed, and there we had some new arrivals who spoke Arabic. I told them that I could speak Arabic. The children and their parents felt lucky to see someone who could speak Arabic with them in their new school. It was another breakthrough for the school management and the teachers because whenever a problem came up, regarding those Italian and Arabic speaking families, I was there to help solve the problems.

The reality is, no matter how easy the problem is, if there is a language barrier, it is nearly impossible to solve it. We also had and still have some Urdu-speaking teachers, who help solve the problems regarding the Urdu-speaking parents and their children. It is really helpful to have multilingual teachers when you have multi-cultural, multi-religious community children in your school.

Many years went by, working with the school when it was the retirement for our headteacher. We all celebrated the invaluable work she had done for the school and the community.

After that, our deputy headteacher took over as the acting headteacher, but later she was appointed as our official head teacher. Since the new headteacher was working in the school for a long time, as a teacher and a deputy headteacher, she came up with some innovative management methods. She made a leading team and team leaders among the teachers, to make sure the work was being done as planned.

Despite not being involved, I could see how things were getting from good to better. Since I am enthusiastic about work, I love to be part of some professional, hardworking staff and their organisation. This made me have confidence in the organisation I work for, and have the mindset of continuing to work with it, until my retirement and beyond.

Many stories took place, regarding the families and their children who were new to the country. Some of them stood out and I couldn't forget them. One of the children was a Korean girl and her mother.

One day, I met the mother and asked her. "From which Korea are you?"

She said, "We are from the middle."

That answer made me laugh, but later I was told the mother was mentally disturbed and the little girl was taken into care. That girl was one of the hardest working children I had seen in the school. She came to the school in her third year with no English language, and after three years in the school, she finished year six in the top group. She was always serious when it came to learning. She stayed in our language support room for a year, and then she was confidently able to cope with her class workload.

At the start of every few years, we as the school staff used to fill in a form called staff appraisal. I remember when I was filling the appraisal form. I wrote what I would like to see happening in the school, especially how I would want to do my job and whom I would want to work with. The head teacher decided to allocate me and another bilingual teaching assistant to work with the new arrivals in a room called Rainbow Retreat. This name reflected the multi-ethnic and multicultural children that we were welcoming and teaching.

Whenever we welcomed some new arrivals, who spoke the languages we speak, it was a delightful moment for the children and their families, because they never expected that they would see some people who spoke their language. We could normally see their faces lit up with joy and appreciation.

In the beginning, the children were quite unsure of how they could start speaking English, but we had already planned some effective basic-English lessons, aimed to help those new arrivals.

I remember a day, when a young boy, who came from Belgium, was brought to our language support room. He could only speak French. I started speaking French with him. The boy and his parents couldn't believe that they found someone who spoke French in a British school. Even for my colleague, it was a surprising moment, because she didn't know how many languages I spoke.

In the morning, the new arrivals were coming into our language support room, feeling relaxed and comfortable. Our daily work went smoothly and the new arrivals were making constant progress.

One afternoon, my Urdu-speaking colleague went to help a teacher who was filling forms for reception children's parents. One of the parents could only speak French and no English at all. The teacher struggled to fill in the form for the French-speaking parent. My Urdu-speaking colleague remembered that I could speak French and told the teacher that I could help her. She sent another teaching assistant to me, to take over my group, while I was helping the teacher to fill in the form. I came in and spoke to the French-speaking parent. She was the mother of the child. She opened her eyes wide with surprise and said, "Vous parlez Français?" which meant "Do you speak French?"

I said, "Oui." Tath meant 'Yes.' Then we started filling the form in with ease. The parent was finally relieved and the teacher thanked me a lot.

For me, it was an achievement and a reward that reminded me of the hard work of learning the languages when I was in Somalia. The stories and the incidents were countless because they were part of our daily jobs.

The school management realised how important it was for the non-English speaking parents to learn how to speak English. Then, they tried to help them. They allocated an afternoon English class for the parents to attend and learn some basic-English lessons. Those lessons were taught by my colleague and I. Most of the parents who needed the lessons were unable to attend, because of the inconvenient timing. However, many were able to attend and benefited from those lessons. Many parents, who learned some English from the beneficial programme, appreciated and thanked the school a lot. They expressed their understanding that the school management was considerate and helpful.

The communication between the school and the parents was consistent and still is. This is because both parts are doing an important job, which is educating the future generation for the country and the world at large. For those parents who could read the English language, it was and still is easy for the school to send English letters and inform them what they needed to know about the school.

Unfortunately, those parents who couldn't read English, needed help and that was and still is when we, the bilingual staff came in to translate the letters into the respective languages. I was translating the letters into the Somali language. Of course, the letters were signed by the management, but when the parents saw it was written in Somali, it immediately reminded them of my presence at the school. They always mentioned it when I met them and appreciated it.

After many years of working in the school, I realised that many families who used to depend on our language translations, became independent because their children became fluent in English and could help their parents. I can imagine how much those parents were relieved from the difficulty they used to endure.

As I mentioned, some stories stood out of the innumerable stories that took place in the school. There were three Palestinian children, who were new arrivals. They were two boys and a girl. They were the same age coming from three different families. Their year group was year five. One afternoon, their teacher wanted to assess the three children's reading ability. The teacher started with the two boys, who were able to read some basic-English words. Then, it was the girl's turn to read. The teacher asked the girl to read the English words. The girl's eyes were closed then she broke into tears. It was that moment when I came in to take the three children to my language support room. To my astonishment, I saw the girl crying with extensive tears in her eyes, standing next to the teacher's desk. I asked the teacher what happened, then, she told me, the girl couldn't read, whereas the boys had read well.

I became emotional and remembered when I was nearly her age, fighting to get an education for myself with a little help in my country. I couldn't hold myself away from the girl and hugged her, rubbing the tears from her eyes. I immediately took her out of the class and promised her that I would teach her how to read and write as soon as possible. She was relieved and felt that the words were coming from her father because I was speaking to her in her mother's language, the Arabic language. There was a big smile on her face that replaced the cry and the tears.

Later, when she went home, she told her parents about what happened that afternoon in the school. The girl started to learn how to read and write. Then very quickly she was able to read. To me, it was quite clear that she was going to do well because it is all about how much willpower you have for what you want to do. Of course, she had tremendous willpower to learn how to read and write. From that day, whenever I saw the girl's parents, there was a big smile on their faces. They were so thankful. The girl and the boys stayed in the school for two years then they moved on to high school. Many years later, I saw the girl's parents in a supermarket in Bolton. They told me their daughter went to university. To me, that was very good news.

When I look at how the community sees how Brandwood Primary School is serving them, it makes me feel proud of what we are doing. Some of the families who perceive the school as the ideal school for their children never look elsewhere for their children. Even those families who used to live near the school, then moved houses to other areas, have decided not to shift their children to the schools near their area.

The other fact that gives me a sense of achievement is that the multi-cultural community of Brandwood School offers an unwavering support which helps us be a happy and harmonious community school.